A Narrative Commentary on Matthew 1–4

When God Walked in Galilee

Discovering Jesus and the Kingdom of Heaven on Earth

RACHEL STARR THOMSON

When God Walked in Galilee: Discovering Jesus and the Kingdom of Heaven on Earth

Published by 1:11 Publishing
An imprint of Little Dozen Press
Crystal Beach, ON, Canada
littledozen.com

Copyright © 2020 by Rachel Starr Thomson

Visit the author at rachelstarrthomson.com.

For bulk order information or for more information about 1:11 Ministries, visit one11ministries.com.

Unless otherwise noted, all Scripture quotations are taken from the Holman Christian Standard Bible®, Copyright © 1999, 2000, 2002, 2003, 2009 by Holman Bible Publishers. Used by permission. Holman Christian Standard Bible®, Holman CSB®, and HCSB® are federally registered trademarks of Holman Bible Publishers.

Scripture quotations marked "NIV" are taken from the Holy Bible, New International Version®, NIV®. Copyright © 1973, 1978, 1984, 2011 by Biblica, Inc.™ Used by permission of Zondervan. All rights reserved worldwide. www.zondervan.com The "NIV" and "New International Version" are trademarks registered in the United States Patent and Trademark Office by Biblica, Inc.™

Scriptures marked "NASB" taken from the New American Standard Bible® (NASB), Copyright © 1960, 1962, 1963, 1968, 1971, 1972, 1973, 1975, 1977, 1995 by The Lockman Foundation. Used by permission. www.Lockman.org

Scriptures marked "ESV" are taken from The ESV® Bible (The Holy Bible, English Standard Version®). ESV® Text Edition: 2016. Copyright © 2001 by Crossway, a publishing ministry of Good News Publishers. The ESV® text has been reproduced in cooperation with and by permission of Good News Publishers. Unauthorized reproduction of this publication is prohibited. All rights reserved.

Scripture quotations marked "ISV" are taken from The Holy Bible: International Standard Version® 2.0. U.S. English Imprint Release 2.0 Copyright © 1996-2012 The ISV Foundation ALL RIGHTS RESERVED INTERNATIONALLY. Used by permission of Davidson Press, LLC. ALL RIGHTS RESERVED INTERNATIONALLY.

Scriptures marked "KJV" are taken from the Holy Bible, King James Version. Public domain.

All Rights Reserved. This book, or any portion thereof, may not be reproduced or transmitted in any form or by any means, electronic or mechanical, including photocopying, recording, or by an information storage and retrieval system (except by a reviewer, who may quote brief passages in a review or other endorsement, or in a recommendation to be printed in a magazine, newspaper, or on the Internet) without written permission from the publisher.

ISBN: 978-1-927658-50-5

Volume 1 of this series contains material adapted from the first seventeen posts on my blog, where I have been blogging verse by verse through the gospel of Matthew since the fall of 2015.

They cover Matthew 1–4. All the original posts (going far beyond this book) can be viewed at: rachelstarrthomson.com/category/gospel-of-matthew.

INTRODUCTION:
The Day When Jesus Heals Everyone

In September 2014 I had a sudden cardiac arrest in a Canadian Tire parking lot. No cause was ever found, but God provided immediate care in the form of a nurse who "just happened" to pull into the parking lot at the very moment that I collapsed. I lived through the experience with minimal damage, though I am told I was technically dead for twelve minutes.

The hospital where I recovered, Hôtel-Dieu Grace Hospital in Windsor, is a merger of two older institutions: Hôtel-Dieu ("hostel of God"), founded by Roman Catholics, and Grace Hospital, founded by the Salvation Army. Although it's government run now, the signs of faith are still everywhere in this hospital and infuse the atmosphere. On the wall in the lobby is a two-story mural of a tree, with the words "The leaves of the tree were for the healing of the nations" (Revelation 22:2). Viewable from a broad window in one of the halls is a garden with another mural: this one a long piece of sculpture, three granite slabs with carved depictions of every healing Jesus performed in the gospels. On those stones, the blind see and the lame leap; paralytics dance and the withered are made whole.

This is how we as the world remember Jesus: as one who healed. Instinctively we know this was more than just a sign of his legitimacy as one sent by God. It was a revelation of his character—of the character of God himself—a signpost of his purpose and desire for the world.

Matthew 4 describes the very beginning of Jesus's ministry:

> Jesus was going all over Galilee, teaching in their synagogues, preaching the good news of the kingdom, and healing every disease and sickness among the people. Then the news about Him spread throughout Syria. So they brought to Him all those who were afflicted, those suffering from various diseases and intense pains, the demon-possessed, the epileptics,[1] and the paralytics. And He healed them. (Matthew 4:23–24)

For me this passage simultaneously offers hope and raises questions. If we will let it, it can shape our entire conception of who God is. This, after all, is our first real glimpse of the incarnation in action: *in human flesh, God heals everyone who comes to him.*

---

[1] Literally "moonstruck"; this word can also be translated "lunatics" or "insane." We can't be 100% sure what group Matthew had in mind when he chose this word.

Healing Physical and Spiritual Brokenness

The story of humanity as the Bible tells it is the story of a beautiful vision marred and broken by a failure of trust and relationship. In the garden of Eden, a perfect world was destroyed by the willingness of human beings to stab God in the back. That brokenness affected all of creation both physically and spiritually in ways we still don't fully understand.

Our brokenness is summed up in the twin problems of sin and death. We "miss the mark" (the literal definition of "sin") and everything dies. That is the curse of our world.

In Matthew's account, "all who were afflicted and suffering" came to Jesus. There are many kinds of affliction and suffering in the world that are not mentioned here, but the kinds that are mentioned function as bookends, framing all the brokenness of creation and human life. At the far physical end, those suffering from disease came to him. At the far spiritual end, the demon-possessed came.

All the rest of our pain lies between those bookends: a combination of physical and spiritual factors that make up the totality of our lives.

Matthew takes time to point out that those who were healed could not even come themselves. These were people so struck down by their afflictions that they had to be brought. He doesn't say who brought them; just that news of what Jesus was doing spread, and the people were brought.

And he healed them.

Jesus Our Healer

Healing was part of Jesus's mission from the beginning, and in the end his whole enterprise will be seen as one of healing—not just of individuals but of the cosmos, the whole world. One of the details that moves me most in this account is that Jesus healed everyone who came to him. This is stated elsewhere in the gospels as well: when people came, when they were brought, Jesus did not turn them away without giving them what they were looking for. He was a generous healer, a no-strings-attached physician. He did not require them to respond to his message first or to follow him afterward. If they had faith enough to come, he healed them.

In a world where it often feels like there isn't enough of what we need to go around, I am profoundly moved by this. They didn't have to earn healing; they didn't have to qualify. They just had to come. Jesus's power and will to heal were abundant.

When John the Baptist questioned whether Jesus was the prophesied messiah, Jesus sent back his resume:

> Go and report to John what you hear and see: the blind see, the lame walk, those with skin diseases are healed, the deaf hear, the

dead are raised, and the poor are told the good news. (Matthew 11:4–5)

What Jesus did locally in Galilee, for a relative handful of people, is intended to eventually release the entire world from the curse of death:

> For the creation eagerly waits with anticipation for God's sons to be revealed. For the creation was subjected to futility—not willingly, but because of Him who subjected it—in the hope that the creation itself will also be set free from the bondage of corruption into the glorious freedom of God's children. (Romans 8:19–21)

GLIMPSES OF THE FUTURE

Jesus still heals today.[2] I have personally witnessed divine healing and know many people who have

---

[2] This is more than a doctrinal stance; there is widespread evidence to support it. "When many Western intellectuals still claim that miracles cannot happen, simply as an unexamined premise, whereas hundreds of millions of people around the world claim to have witnessed just such events, some in indisputably dramatic ways, I believe that genuinely open-minded academicians should reexamine our presuppositions with an open mind … While eyewitness claims do not constitute indisputable proof, they do constitute evidence that may be considered rather than a priori dismissed." (Craig Keener, *"Introduction," Miracles: The Credibility of the New Testament Accounts*, Vol 1, 2. Grand Rapids: Baker Academic, 2011.) Keener's book is a two-volume, 1248-page discussion of miracle claims within global Christianity today and in the past, including the arguments for and against their validity as supernatural events.

experienced it. The heart and power of God to heal our brokenness—all forms of brokenness—remains.

At the same time, I know many people who have prayed for healing and not received it. The New Testament indicates that this was the case for the early church as well: while healings and miracles did continue into the apostolic era, we get glimpses in Paul's letters especially that universal healing wasn't expected, and some Christians (including probably Paul himself) suffered from illness and physical ailments that were not miraculously healed.

Some today place all the "blame" for this at the door of those who are sick or those who are praying: somebody doesn't have enough faith. But given the testimony of the New Testament, I don't think that's a right view. Rather, healing is meant to point forward to Jesus's ultimate purpose as the King who brings heaven to earth and reconciles the two. Healing now is a signpost of the future.

I don't have all the answers as to why some are healed and some are not, but I believe in the heart of the God-Man seen in Matthew, and I know that his mission is to heal all our brokenness, completely and forever, in the end.

Everyone and everything dies, and that is the curse of our world. The consummation of Jesus's mission is the resurrection, when those who are in

Christ will be physically resurrected, never to die again. Healings now are like bursts of that future resurrection coming into the present: down payments in a sense, or foretastes, of the day the curse is entirely halted and creation is set fully free. In this cosmic and eternal sense, ALL who come to Jesus for healing will be healed, as they were in Galilee. But this time corruption will never get the better of them again.

The mural in the lobby at Hôtel-Dieu Grace Hospital looks forward to that day:

> And he shewed me a pure river of water of life, clear as crystal, proceeding out of the throne of God and of the Lamb. In the midst of the street of it, and on either side of the river, was there the tree of life ... and the leaves of the tree were for the healing of the nations. (Revelation 22:1–2, KJV)

The Kingdom of God Is at Hand

When John the Baptist started heralding the arrival of Jesus over two thousand years ago, it was with the declaration "Repent, for the kingdom of God is at hand."

Jesus kicked off his ministry at the age of thirty with the same words.

The whole Bible, in fact, leads up to and then

underscores this reality-altering fact: The kingdom of God is here.

And, at the same time, we still pray every day: *Your kingdom come.*

Growing up in the church, I never really heard much about the kingdom until I was a teenager and became part of a ministry out in the desert where the kingdom was talked about a lot. It seemed important to differentiate between "the kingdom" and "the church," and between the gospel of the kingdom preached by Jesus and the more Sunday school version of the gospel preached by most evangelicals.

On some level I believed this was true. The kingdom was important. But I still didn't know what it was. And my mentors in ministry never really defined it.

Ever since, I've been on a journey of trying to comprehend—and live well within—the kingdom of God.

In the course of the journey, I've learned this kingdom is biblical, historical, spiritual, and personal. It impacts everything. It touches everyone. It runs through the entire Bible and makes sense out of Jesus and his life and his mission and the church, today—us and our lives and our mission.

And in seeking to understand the kingdom, I've learned that I need to better understand the King. In fact, King and kingdom are so closely linked they are nearly interchangeable. It was the gospel of Matthew, an ancient book which serves as something of a bridge between Old and New Testaments, that first helped me begin to understand. And in the pages of this gospel, I discovered Jesus all over again.

This book, which covers the first four chapters of the gospel of Matthew, is about the King and the kingdom. It aims to reintroduce us to the King through the context of his early life and ministry and to pull back the veil that often obscures our reading by delving into the Old Testament roots of the story Matthew tells. In the process, in seeing Jesus and his story afresh, we are given the opportunity to see ourselves afresh as well. After all, the kingdom story is about God, and it's about us. It's about our place in a reality that came out of the grave with Jesus over two millennia ago and has been changing our world—from the inside out—ever since.

I'm excited to dive in with you.

Ready?

Great. Let's go.

THE RECORD OF THE GENEALOGY OF JESUS
THE MESSIAH, THE SON OF DAVID,
THE SON OF ABRAHAM.

(Matthew 1:1, NASB)

1

Anointed One: The King and His Mission

We are citizens in the kingdom of God.

But do we know who our King is?

I'm asking that question seriously, because honestly, many of us in the world of modern Christianity have gotten so used to reading the Bible as "life's little instruction book" that we've forgotten it's a story. A history. A history that centers around a person, a man who became king and who is sitting now on the throne of the kingdom of heaven.

A man with a family, a history, a mission, and a role in the universe that affects us all.

I just want to say up front: the Bible is the most loaded book I have ever read. You can spend hours picking apart just one phrase. Matthew 1:1 is a case in point. When I started teaching a Bible study through Matthew some time ago, I spent over an hour on this one verse, and I only scratched the surface.

One verse. Four phrases. Seventeen words—not one of them wasted. Every word drips with significance: historical background, prophetic allusion, and declaration of who this man is and what he came to do.

Here, he says, is the record of the genealogy (the "book of the genesis" in Greek, and yes—that too is an allusion) of the man Jesus.

Jesus was born a Jew, into two particular lines of promise: the line of blessing and the line of kingship. He was (and is) the direct heir of two enormously significant covenants, promised first to Israel and then, through that nation, to the entire world.

But I'm jumping ahead.

"This is the record of the genealogy."

That phrase all by itself means that Jesus is not like other gods. He's not a myth or a fairy tale. He's a *man*, one who could look up his family tree on Genealogy.com. *This is the record of the genealogy*. He was born in the real world, in a real place, at a real time, to a real family.

But then he's called Jesus.

The name is the Greek form of Yeshua, Joshua in English, which means "Yahweh saves."

Prophetic, yes. Allusive, yes. Pointing to Jesus's identity as Yahweh incarnate, yes.

And then Matthew also calls him the Messiah, Christ in Greek, which literally means "Anointed One."

In the Old Testament world that laid the foundations for Jesus's coming, being anointed with oil signified being given authority in the service of God. It wasn't a common ceremony. Priests, prophets, and kings were anointed. It signified their right and responsibility to fulfill their roles with God's power and blessing.

The Role and Responsibility of Jesus

Jesus had a very specific mission that came with his anointing. It remains his mission today—one we share as his body in the world. (But that's jumping waaaay ahead.)

He declared it himself when he began his ministry, reading the ancient words of Isaiah:

> The Spirit of the Lord GOD is on Me,
> because the LORD has anointed Me
> to bring good news to the poor.
> He has sent Me to heal
> the brokenhearted,
> to proclaim liberty to the captives
> and freedom to the prisoners;
> to proclaim the year
> of the LORD's favor,

> and the day of our God's vengeance;
> to comfort all who mourn in Zion;
> to give them a crown of beauty
> instead of ashes,
> festive oil instead of mourning,
> and splendid clothes
> instead of despair.
> And they will be called righteous trees,
> planted by the LORD to glorify Him.
> (Isaiah 61:1–3)

This man Matthew introduces is Yeshua HaMashiach, Yeshua the Messiah, Jesus Christ. Yahweh who saves and who was promised. The man who has come into the world full of the Spirit of the Lord, anointed and appointed to bring good news, to heal the brokenhearted, free the captives, turn mourning into dancing, and clothe the despairing human race in glory.

His mission is to make of you and me "trees of righteousness, planted by the LORD." Full of God's own life and manifesting that life in the world through the fruit we bear.

That is the Jesus Matthew announced.

But I do have to wonder if it's the Jesus many of us know. Because quite honestly, often I think we don't really know what Jesus's mission is at all—what he's anointed, empowered, and desirous to do.

What Salvation Truly Means

According to the Scriptures, Jesus came to save. Before we whitewash that word saved until it doesn't mean anything that really means anything, let's break it down. The Greek word we translate "salvation," *soteria*, means to rescue from danger or trouble. It's also translated "deliverance," and it extends to rescue of all sorts—from one's enemies, from hunger and disease, from judgment or anger, from calamity, from prison, from the power of sin, from national oppression.

As part of his overall rescue mission for humanity, Jesus drew his more specific mission statement from Isaiah 61. When we say we trust Jesus to "save" us, then, we proclaim that our faith is in one who has come:

- to bring good news

- to heal

- to comfort

- to proclaim liberty

- to announce God's favor and also God's vengeance, on his enemies (and on ours)

- to exchange beauty for ashes, joy for sorrow, glory for despair.

Salvation is not simply a matter of escaping the world after death. It is holistic, and it is now (and also later). Jesus has come to make us fully alive, where before we were withering and all but dead. He has come to plant us by living waters and manifest his righteousness and his life through us. That is salvation.

"Righteousness," by the way, should not be read merely as "morality" in a narrow or restrictive sense. In biblical terms, to be righteous is to be just and right on a fundamental level. It is to be in conformity with the nature and will of God, which nature and will themselves gave shape to the universe and all that is in it. From that angle, to be righteous is to be fully aligned with reality as God designed and envisioned it from the start. It is to be fully human and fully alive. Righteousness is whole and healthy; it combats that in our souls which is corrupt and diseased, and by extension it combats the broken and evil in the world cultures we give birth to. In a sense righteousness has a creative energy within it, a life force—when we are personally righteous, we effect the "right-making" of the world.

For some time and for many reasons Christians have shaved away the holistic and life-affirming dimensions of their faith in favor of a highly spiritualized (the technical word is "dualistic") form of "salvation" that is all about the afterlife, and which makes ideas like sanctification seem like an oddly irrelevant tacked-on burden extraneous to being saved. But this is unfortunate for many reasons, not least of which that it's actually Christianity's holistic, life-embracing nature that sets it apart from other forms of "spirituality," which view the ultimate goal of life as detachment and escape. Jesus was (and is) on a mission to meet all of the crying needs of mankind, not to tell us we don't really need those things after all; to make our deepest heart's desires come true, not to warn us against wanting anything; and to glorify us so we will glorify him.

If you're going to serve a king, it's good to know what he's all about. What his mission is.

Not least because we need saving.

And not least because, when we get caught up with Jesus and become part of his kingdom, salvation becomes our mission too.

The historical record
of Jesus Christ ...
(Matthew 1:1a, HCSB)

2

How We Make God in Our Image . . . and How We Can Know Who He Really Is

When the children of Israel came out of the desert and God made a covenant with them, his very first two commands were these: *You shall have no other gods before me* and *You shall make for yourself no graven image*—no idols.

The interesting thing is they weren't in all that much danger of making graven images of other gods. They were in danger of making one of Yahweh.

When Aaron made the golden calf, he said, "This is Yahweh, your god who brought you out of Egypt." When Moses made a bronze serpent and lifted it up in the wilderness at God's command, it accomplished God's purpose in its time—but a few hundred years later, the people started worshiping it, and Hezekiah had to destroy it.

We do this too.

We take the materials of our lives, our experience, and our broken sinfulness, and we use them to construct an image of God.

So if we are harsh and unforgiving, we think God is harsh and unforgiving.

If we are legalists, God is a legalist.

If our parents were too busy for us, God is too busy for us.

If our husband walked out on us, or nobody ever wanted us, we think God will abandon us or never want us in the first place.

We think God is a workaholic who would like to work us into the grave. We think he's stingy and penny-pinching.

If we've experienced a lot of control and manipulation, then God's "love" is a code word for control and manipulation.

(Just a sidenote: if you really love the Lord and you seek to obey him, do you think God wants your loyalty and love, even in your imperfections, or do you think he wants your puppet strings so he can jerk you around and ensure you'll never make a mistake? Your answer to this question says a great deal about how you view God's love.)

We hold onto many of these mistaken beliefs about God even after we become believers. I speak as one who knows. We think God is an egomaniac, he's selfish, he's controlling, he's abusive.

He's still our only way to be saved, and we know he's the best thing in the universe, so we love him, and we try hard to surrender and be good Christians.

But I'll tell you this: as much as I think he appreciates our efforts to surrender even when we're surrendering to a distorted idea of who he is and what he wants, our God would rather we got rid of our graven images and learned to know him as he really is.

That's why I asked, in the previous chapter: Do we know who our king is?

Do we really know him? Do we know why he came—his mission and ours? Do we know what he's really like?

When Moses asked God for his name, he told him, "I AM THAT I AM." The Hebrew word for this is transliterated into English as "Yahweh" or "Jehovah."

The name is a riddle. A mystery.

In John 17:6, Jesus said:

> I have revealed Your name
> to the men you gave Me.

Jesus has unlocked the riddle. That's why he could tell Philip, "If you have seen Me, you have seen the Father" (John 14:9). Jesus has revealed the Name. That's why the gospel of John is full of "I am" statements.

Do we know God this way?

> *"I am the Good Shepherd."*
>
> *"I am the Bread of Life . . . I am the living bread that came down from heaven."*
>
> *"I am the resurrection and the life."*
>
> *"I am the light of the world."*
>
> *"I am the way, the truth, and the life."*
>
> *"I am the Vine."*
>
> *"I am the door."*

My deepest desire is to know the answers to the riddle of the Name myself. I want to know Jesus the way he really is.

The thing that really moves me, though—that makes me tremble and get all teary-eyed?

That Jesus is so much better than I would make him.

In my life, and in yours, may the graven images crumble before the Great I Am.

The historical record of Jesus Christ,
the Son of David, the Son of Abraham
... So all the generations from
Abraham to David were 14 generations;
and from David until the exile
to Babylon, 14 generations;
and from the exile to Babylon
until the Messiah, 14 generations.

(Matthew 1:1, 17)

3

Son of Blessing, Son of Kings: Why Jesus Is the Gateway to Life

The question raised by this first verse still stands: *Do we know who our King is?*

Unlike Luke, who traces Jesus all the way back to Adam, Matthew starts with Abraham. As he lays out the genealogy of Christ in verses 2–16 (following an interesting, deliberate, and controversial pattern), he highlights David, the Babylonian exile, and the number 14.[1]

Whatever else may be going on there, Matthew is deliberately placing Christ in the line of covenant history. As we will see in a moment, Abraham and David are significant not just because they were

---

1   It's entirely possible Matthew coded the entire genealogy as an allusion-rich riddle underscoring Jesus's identity as the long-awaited Messiah and as the "new man" created in his resurrection. I came across this idea through William Struse, who has been laying it out in a series of fiction and nonfiction books as well as on his blog. Check it all out, in fiction or nonfiction form, at The13thEnumeration.com.

men of faith who passed their genes along to Jesus but because each man received a covenant from God of which Jesus is the heir and fulfillment.

He is the Son of Blessing and the Son of Kings.

This matters for us. Not only because we need to understand who Jesus is, but because in a twist we will continually revisit, who *we are* is dependent on who Jesus is. He has designed things so that our identity and destiny are tied up with his. If he suffers, so will we. If he is a harbinger of blessing, so are we. If he is a king, we too must rule.

"If we suffer, we shall also reign with him," Paul declares. "We are the children of God: and if children, then heirs; heirs of God, and joint-heirs with Christ . . . As he is, so are we in this world." And again, we are "his body, the fulness of him that filleth all in all."[2]

Matthew 1:1 presents us with more than just a family history. Matthew is showing us the sum and the point and the heart of everything.

Blessings and Covenants

Covenant history is often said to begin with Abraham, and more specifically, with the blessing of Abraham. From the beginning, God has covenanted with human beings in order to bless them.

---

[2] 2 Timothy 2:12, Romans 8:16–17, 1 John 4:17, Ephesians 1:23 (King James Version)

The story goes like this: Some generations after mankind fell into sin, creation was cursed, and Death took up its tyrannical reign over life, a mostly-forgotten Creator God struck up a friendship with a man in the Ancient Near East named Abraham.

He made a covenant with him and promised him something incredible:

> Get thee out of thy country, and from thy kindred, and from thy father's house, unto a land that I will show thee: and I will make of thee a great nation, and I will bless thee, and make thy name great; and thou shalt be a blessing: and I will bless them that bless thee, and curse him that curseth thee: and in thee shall all families of the earth be blessed. (Genesis 12:1–3, KJV)

Millennia later, Paul wrote about this promise. He saw in it an expanded promise: Abraham was to be "heir of the cosmos"—and not only Abraham, but all who qualify as his children by virtue of their faith:

> For the promise to Abraham or to his descendants that he would inherit the world [Greek: cosmos] was not through the law, but through the righteousness that comes by faith. (Romans 4:13)

In a curse-bound world, God promised blessing.

Blessings and Curses

From the beginning, God's purpose, through covenant, has been to bless. What does that mean?

A study through the Bible passages that use the word *blessing*, Hebrew *barak*, shows it to be the source of life, righteousness, prosperity, and salvation.

Fundamentally, to bless is to fill with the capacity and potential for life.

To curse is the opposite—it is to wither, dry up, make barren.

Blessing is a kind of empowerment given through the spoken word of God. It is as significant to human origins as creation itself. Immediately after creating mankind, God blessed them. For this reason, we have the power to create and to procreate: to bring forth life and to prosper. And for the same reason, because we are blessed by God as his image-bearers and vice-regents in the earth, we are empowered to be more than animals or plants. For good or for ill, we create, we rule, we influence through our wills and actions. We are creatures of real significance—because we are blessed.

And we are kept in check because we are cursed—because we die.

("If they should live forever —" God says in Genesis 3:22. And although we usually finish it in English for the sake of a clear translation, in Hebrew the thought cuts off, because the idea of sinful man living forever is too terrible to contemplate.)

The original blessing went awry when man fell. But God was not satisfied with that fallen state of affairs. And so he came to Abraham and promised him blessing upon blessing, until at last "all families of the earth" would be blessed "in him" as he became heir not simply of a patch of ground in the Middle East but of the whole world.

In its typical "already but not yet" fashion, the Bible traces that blessing through Abraham to his descendants in Isaac, then Jacob, then the nation of Israel, and finally to Jesus, announced by Matthew as "the Son of Abraham."

Through Jesus, the blessing of Abraham—life, salvation, prosperity, healing, creative power, influence, righteousness—comes on all the children of faith.

> And ye be Christ's, then are ye Abraham's seed, and heirs according to the promise . . . wherefore thou art no more a servant, but a son; and if a son, then an heir of God through Christ. (Galatians 3:29, 4:7, KJV)

The Kingdom Covenant

Jesus is also the Son of Kings. Matthew identifies him in the first verse of his gospel as "the son of David."

David, the shepherd boy who killed a giant with a sling and a stone, is one of the best-known figures in the Bible, even to those outside of the household of faith. Who hasn't heard of David and Goliath? But in Scripture's long story of kingdoms and covenants, David is far more than a giant-slayer. He is the first of the kingly line that unites the throne of God with the throne of man. Put another way, after the fall of Adam, David was the first human king in the kingdom of God.

When God delivered the people of Israel out of Egypt, he declared his intention to be their king (see Exodus 19:5–6 and Deuteronomy 33:5). The people of Israel were the kingdom of God, with God's personal rule manifested and delegated to them through a series of judges. But God also knew they would eventually want a human king "like all the other nations" (see Deuteronomy 17:14–20), and in a brilliant and beautiful show of divine humility and cunning, he answered their desire by giving them the family of David—while simultaneously plotting to be born into that family in due time and put himself directly back on the throne.

The Forever King

Israel's first king, demanded prematurely, was Saul. But in the ancient world as today, kingship remains in a family only so long as no other family rises up to replace it. So David, chosen and anointed by God through the last judge, Samuel, replaced Saul. The kingdom of Israel would later split into separate Northern and Southern kingdoms called Israel and Judah, with David's family reigning over the Southern Kingdom of Judah alone, but God made a promise and covenant with David concerning his family line:

> This is what the LORD of hosts says: "I took you from the pasture and from following the sheep to be ruler over My people Israel . . . I declare to you that the LORD Himself will build a house for you. When your time comes to be with your fathers, I will raise up after you your descendant, who is one of your own sons, and I will establish his kingdom. He will build a house for Me, and I will establish His throne forever. I will be a father to him, and he will be a son to Me. I will not take away My faithful love from him as I took it from the one who was before you. I will appoint him over My house and My kingdom forever, and his throne will be established forever." (1 Chronicles 17:7, 11–14)

Throughout the tumultuous history that followed, the promise of David's ever-reigning Son stands out in prophecy as the great hope of Israel and the nations. Who hasn't heard the words of Isaiah?

> For unto us a son is born,
> unto us a son is given,
> and the government shall be upon his shoulder:
> And his name shall be called Wonderful, Counselor, The mighty God,
> The everlasting Father, The Prince of Peace.
> Of the increase of his government and peace there shall be no end,
> upon the throne of David, and upon his kingdom,
> to order it, and to establish it with judgment and with justice
> from henceforth even for ever.
> The zeal of the LORD of hosts will perform this.
> (Isaiah 9:6–7, KJV)

In the Southern Kingdom of Judah, David's sons remained on the throne in an unbroken line until the exile to Babylon—the third division marked by Matthew in his genealogy of Jesus Christ.

> So all the generations from Abraham to David were 14 generations; and from David un-

> til the exile to Babylon, 14 generations; and
> from the exile to Babylon until the Messiah,
> 14 generations. (Matthew 1:17)

The exile also marked the official coming of the "curse of the law" upon Israel. The Mosaic Law was a treaty-style covenant with Israel, containing both blessings for faithfulness to the covenant and curses for breaking it. The last and greatest curse was total exile from the promised land. By the time of the Babylonian captivity, the people of Israel had been guilty of unfaithfulness to God for hundreds of years. At long last, he brought the curse upon them.

The people of blessing, trapped under a curse.

The kingdom of God, haunted by an empty throne.

So Matthew's genealogy, with its touchpoints at Abraham, David, and the exile, highlights the promises of God, their terrible reversals because of human rebellion, and then the reversal of all reversals when Jesus arrives on the scene.

The Son of Abraham comes to bring the blessing at last, marking a new era of life, prosperity, and creative power. The Son of David comes to rule with justice, judgment, and astonishing light. God returns to his people. The people are given the opportunity to return to God. With the coming of Jesus, exile is over.

Jesus did not arrive on the scene of human history out of nowhere. He didn't come in a vacuum. Rather, as Paul put it, he came "in the fullness of time" (Galatians 4:4) as the fulfillment of a plan God had been putting into place, piece by piece and promise by promise, for thousands of years.

> In those days came John the Baptist, preaching in the wilderness of Judea, and saying, "Repent ye: for the kingdom of heaven is at hand!" For this is he that was spoken of by the prophet Isaiah, saying, The voice of one crying in the wilderness, Prepare ye the way of the Lord, make his paths straight. (Matthew 3:1–3, KJV)

It is all of this history that tells us who our King is and hints at what he's come to do. He is the Wonderful Counselor, the Mighty God, the Everlasting Father, the Prince of Peace. His story is bigger than we may realize at first glance. And God's kingdom, and his desire to bless us with abundant life and to walk in our midst, are right at the heart of it.

All of this history will bring us to the day the herald, John the Baptist, arrives on the scene with his galvanizing cry: "Repent, for the kingdom of heaven is at hand!"

But first, before the herald, the King had to be born.

The birth of Jesus Christ came about this way: After Mary his mother had been engaged to Joseph, it was discovered before they came together that she was pregnant by the Holy Spirit. So her husband Joseph, being a righteous man, and not wanting to disgrace her publicly, decided to divorce her secretly. But after he had considered these things, an angel of the Lord suddenly appeared to him in a dream, saying, "Joseph, son of David, don't be afraid to take Mary as your wife, because what has been conceived in her is by the Holy Spirit. She will give birth to a son, and you are to name Him Jesus, because He will save His people from their sins." Now all this took place to fulfill what was spoken by the Lord through the prophet:

"See, the virgin will become pregnant and give birth to a son, and they will name Him Immanuel."

(Matthew 1:18–23)

4

Name Him Jesus, Call Him Immanuel: The Names of Jesus and the Point of Religion

They named him Jesus—Yahweh Saves.

They called him Immanuel—God With Us.

God, our Creator, become one of us.

God, our Deliverer, enacting salvation by himself and in himself.

> *(He saw that there was no man,*
>   *and wondered that there was no one to intercede;*
> *then his own arm brought him salvation,*
>   *and his righteousness upheld him.*
> *He put on righteousness as a breastplate,*
>   *and a helmet of salvation on his head;*
> *he put on garments of vengeance for clothing,*
>   *and wrapped himself in zeal as a cloak.*
> *Isaiah 59:16–17, ESV)*

Jesus is Son of God become Son of Man, eternally blurring the lines of separation between God and humanity.

> *(Jesus said to him, "Have I been with you so long, and you still do not know me, Philip? Whoever has seen me has seen the Father." John 14:9, ESV)*

Jesus is the Son of David sitting on the throne of the kingdom of God forever, because he is himself God even as he is himself man and son of David's line. Hundreds of years before, God promised David that a son of his would sit on the throne forever. Then God ensured that he himself was born into David's line. It is beautiful, cosmic sleight of hand. It is God keeping his promises to us by making sure that it's all on himself to do it.

> *(Your throne, O God, is forever and ever.*
> *The scepter of your kingdom is a scepter of uprightness;*
> *you have loved righteousness and hated wickedness.*
> *Therefore God, your God, has anointed you*
> *with the oil of gladness beyond your companions.*
> *Psalm 45:6-7, ESV)*

We're told often that all religions are the same. That if you dig deep enough, you'll find they share the same core, making everything else just chaff. But that is a fundamental misunderstanding of what Christianity, at least, is.

Yes, if you dig deep enough, you'll find that most religions share a core system of moral values. Of course, you'll find that most *humans* share that core system, regardless of religious beliefs. C.S. Lewis unfolded this brilliantly in his classic *Mere Christianity*. Pretty much all of us think it's wrong to steal, murder, cheat on your spouse, etc.—at least when someone's doing it to us. But that isn't what Christianity is about. Morals are important. But they are not the point.

The point is who Jesus is.

The point is that YAHWEH SAVES—not our efforts, our rituals, our spirituality, our good deeds.

The point is a Person who desires relationship.

The point is that salvation *is* a relationship.

Relationship with God is salvation.

Jesus is God with us.

He is the Creator returned to his creation and in fact immersed in it.

He is invisible Spirit forever dressed in skin and bones.

This bears pondering far more than we ponder it. It bears wondering at. The incarnation. The central mystery of our faith.

The prophet Ezekiel looked into heaven and saw a Man on the throne (Ezekiel 8:2).

This is what the kingdom of God means. God is a man, on the throne of his kingdom forever. A Man is God, ruling eternally as a representative of the human race.

Trust in Jesus—in Yahweh Saves.

Walk with Immanuel—with God With Us.

After Jesus was born in Bethlehem of Judea in the days of King Herod, wise men from the east arrived unexpectedly in Jerusalem, saying, "Where is He who has been born King of the Jews? For we saw His star in the east and have come to worship Him."

(Matthew 2:1–2)

5

Magi: The Riddle of Reality and the Mystery Men from the East

The whole story of the coming of the Magi to worship the infant Jesus is told in Matthew 2:1–12. Thanks to crèches and Christmas carols, it is one of history's most iconic scenes.

For me it calls to mind another well-known passage of Scripture, this one from the prophet Isaiah:

> Arise, shine, for your light has come,
>   and the glory of the Lord has risen upon you.
> For behold, darkness shall cover the earth,
>   and thick darkness the peoples;
> but the Lord will arise upon you,
>   and his glory will be seen upon you.
> And nations shall come to your light,
>   and kings to the brightness of your rising.
> Lift up your eyes all around, and see;

> they all gather together, they come to you;
> your sons shall come from afar,
> > and your daughters shall be carried on the hip.
> Then you shall see and be radiant;
> > your heart shall thrill and exult,
> because the abundance of the sea shall be turned to you,
> > the wealth of the nations shall come to you . . .
> They shall bring gold and frankincense,
> > and shall bring good news, the praises of the Lord.
>
> (Isaiah 60:1–6)

We celebrate it every Christmas, and therefore the story suffers from overfamiliarity. But the arrival of the Magi is one of the most strange, mysterious, and prophetically fraught events in the birth narrative of Jesus Christ—and in all of history, really. There's so much Matthew never explains about these men. He calls them *Magoi* in Greek—"Magi" or "wise men," as it's sometimes translated. They were Gentiles "from the east," who claimed they had seen a star rise that announced the birth of the king of the Jews, and they had come to worship him.

On every possible level, this is a strange story. Like everything else in Matthew, its surface simplicity lies over a reality full of riddles: this is layered, and the deeper we go, the stranger and more wonderful and revelatory the story becomes.

Although tradition has turned these men into "kings" and brought them from various parts of the world, historically the Magi seem to have been members of the ancient priestly caste of the Medes and Persians, a group that came into power prior to the Babylonian empire and remained in power throughout the empires to come. The Magi are encountered in the book of Daniel serving as his fellow "magicians." In fact, it's very possible they learned to watch for the "king of Jews," the Messiah, from Daniel. They were politically powerful monotheistic priests, astronomers, astrologers, and—perhaps most importantly for this story—kingmakers.[1]

As we have seen, Matthew uses his opening genealogy to place Jesus squarely at the center of Jewish history, from the blessing of Abraham to the everlasting throne of David and through the exile to the prophesied time of renewal. But the blessing of Abraham had always been intended to extend to all nations, and the reestablished throne of David was to one day draw the nations of the world to God. The prophets who warned Israel of the coming ex-

---

[1] See John MacArthur, "Who Were the Wise Men?", Grace to You sermon, https://www.gty.org/library/sermons-library/2182/who-were-the-wise-men

ile also promised them an eventual influence that would extend to all nations as the Gentiles flocked to them, to learn from God and worship him.[2]

> On that day the root of Jesse
> will stand as a banner for the peoples.
> The nations will seek Him,
> and His resting place will be glorious.
> (Isaiah 11:1)

The Magi are a startling and literal firstfruits of this promise. Somehow, someway, these men—however many there actually were—saw what the rest of the world could not yet see: that the Jewish child born in a stable in Bethlehem was a king for the world and a God to be worshiped. They brought him the wealth of the nations: gold, frankincense, myrrh.[3] And they foreshadowed the millennia to come, in which multitudes of Gentiles would see in the Jewish Messiah their King, their Savior, their Lord.

All of this for a squalling baby in a feeding trough.

It's incredible to ponder that they knew. That somehow, God revealed to them who this child really was and prompted them to walk in fulfilment

---

[2] See Isaiah 11:10, Isaiah 60:3, Micah 4:1–3
[3] Isaiah 60:5–6 prophesied in detail that would this be done on a larger scale, even naming frankincense and gold specifically as gifts to be brought by the nations.

of ancient prophecies given to people of another nation.

To me, the Magi are a reminder that much of reality is a riddle, that the truth is something deeper and more wonderful than we can necessarily see on the surface. They remind me that to understand what is in front of me, I need more than the sight of my eyes. I need divine revelation and guidance, imperfect though my understanding of it may be—the kind that comes from knowing someone like Daniel; the kind that comes from following a star.

The infant in Bethlehem did not look like a king when the Magi found him, yet they recognized him for what he was. Today the King still chooses to cloak himself, to remain hidden and gentle so that people may seek him, find him, come to him. We too need divine sight to see who he truly is.

The Magi remind me as well that God's plans are greater, more generous, and more far-reaching than I tend to believe. My own mind tries to narrow God down, to wrestle him into a shape that makes sense to me. But the King of Israel was in fact the King of the World. The One who later resisted being crowned king of the Jews by his own people was visited first by the kingmakers of the Medes and Persians—by pagan astrologers. This one visit reveals that God had been at work for centuries among people outside the pale; that the web of his weaving extended far beyond Israel, just as it extends far beyond my church, my denomination, my limited understanding. The seeds God planted with Daniel did not die; they were not forgotten; they grew.

And I'm humbled by the faith of men who laid riches down at the feet of an infant. Who recognized in such offensively humble beginnings the source of blessing and prosperity for the whole world.

The Magi cause me to worship a God who is greater and more mysterious than I know and to ask that the Lord will open my eyes to the riddles that lie before me, written on the pages of the Bible, riding in the sky, incarnate in the human beings indwelt by God with whom I live and interact every day. Life is a divine riddle cloaked in humble, ordinary, and unexpected things.

Now and again, the answers to the riddle are revealed to be astonishing.

> It shall come to pass in the latter days
>   that the mountain of the house of the LORD
> shall be established as the highest of the mountains,
>   and it shall be lifted up above the hills;
> and peoples shall flow to it,
>   and many nations shall come, and say:
> "Come, let us go up to the mountain of the LORD,

    to the house of the God of Jacob,
that he may teach us his ways
    and that we may walk in his paths."
For out of Zion shall go forth the law,
    and the word of the LORD from Jerusalem.
(Micah 4:1–2, ESV)

After they were gone, an angel of the Lord suddenly appeared to Joseph in a dream, saying, "Get up! Take the child and His mother, flee to Egypt, and stay there until I tell you. For Herod is about to search for the child to destroy Him." So he got up, took the child and His mother during the night, and escaped to Egypt. He stayed there until Herod's death, so that what was spoken by the Lord through the prophet might be fulfilled: Out of Egypt I called My Son.

(Matthew 2:13–15)

6

Out of Egypt: When God Calls You to Leave Slavery Behind

So far in the first chapter of Matthew, Matthew has identified Jesus with Abraham, with David, and with the people of Israel in exile—and of course, he has identified him clearly as the Anointed One, the "Messiah"; and with Yahweh himself. But there is still more to who Jesus is, in a prophetic and personal sense.

Here, where Matthew tells the story of Jesus's childhood sojourn in Egypt, he identifies him with the nation of Israel.

This identification of the nation with the Messiah, as though the Messiah encompasses the destiny and purpose of the entire nation within himself, is accomplished in multiple places throughout the Bible. For Matthew, the identification begins here, when he quotes Hosea 11:1, "Out of Egypt I called my son," and says that Jesus's return to Palestine after his parents fled with him to Egypt is somehow fulfilled in this Scripture.

It's a fascinating citation on multiple levels. For one thing, in its original context in Hosea, the statement does not appear to be a prophecy. Nor would anyone reading it in Hosea have understood it to mean God would call his literal son out of Egypt. In the Old Testament, the statement is clearly a reflection on the past, when God brought the people of Israel out of Egypt under Moses.

But rather than being problematic ("We can't trust the Bible! The gospel writers are playing fast and loose with the Old Testament!"), Matthew's statement highlights how fully Jesus comes as the fulfillment not only of specific prophecies *but of all the types and shadows of the Old Testament.*

> Typology is a special kind of symbolism. (A symbol is something which represents something else.) We can define a type as a "prophetic symbol" because all types are representations of something yet future. More specifically, a type in scripture is a person or thing in the Old Testament which foreshadows a person or thing in the New Testament. For example, the flood of Noah's day (Genesis 6–7) is used as a type of baptism in 1 Peter 3:20–21.[1]

---

[1] "What Is Biblical Typology?" Got Questions Ministries, https://www.gotquestions.org/typology-Biblical.html

Jesus comes as the fullness of every Old Testament type. He is the body whose shadow, cast back over history, was seen for centuries.

Finding Ourselves in the Pattern

Jesus lived out the patterns of the Old Testament in sometimes startling ways. His story was woven into history before the universe began. But as his people, we also walk in the patterns of his life, finding our own place in the story the whole world keeps telling, over and over again.

Out of Egypt, God called his Son. And out of Egypt, he calls us too.

Egypt represents so many things in Old Testament typology.

First, of course, it represents slavery. We are delivered from sin and the devil's oppression in the same way the Israelites were delivered from slavery to human oppressors.

Second, Egypt represents a lesser revelation of God. During their time in Egypt, the Israelites knew about God through the promises given to their forefathers Abraham, Isaac, and Jacob, and through a handful of stories about God's dealings with those forefathers. But they didn't have anything close to the revelation that came with the first exodus: the fire on the mountain, the blazing holiness of God, the detailed teachings and instructions of the law, the signs and wonders and shattering miracles.

In the exodus God revealed himself as the Almighty God, as God *alone,* so much greater than the gods of Egypt as to belong to an entirely different class (or more accurately, as to constitute a class all his own). He revealed himself as holy and jealous and as the only Lord of Life and Death.

In the same way, when we're called out of sin and slavery, we're also called into a fuller revelation of God. This is the revelation that came with Jesus—a revelation of God as redeemer and seeker of the lost, as the sacrificial Lamb, as the Lord who loves his people to the death and back again. Jesus's coming also led to the revelation of the indwelling Holy Spirit: the intensely personal God, the Lord of the universe who quite literally moves into our inmost being and fellowships with us there.

Coming to know this God is an eternal pursuit. "This is eternal life," Jesus said, "that you know God and Jesus Christ, whom he has sent" (John 17:3).

Out of Egypt

When the people of Israel originally went to Egypt, they were seeking provision in a time of famine. Egypt was a refuge for them. It didn't become a place of slavery until several generations later. Mirroring this, Jesus's family fled to Egypt when he was an infant to seek safety. Herod sought the baby's life, and Joseph was warned in a dream to flee to Egypt, and so he did.

But just as the Israelites could not realize their ultimate purpose as God's people while they remained in Egypt, Jesus could not have fulfilled his destiny as Israel's Messiah had his family stayed in Egypt long term. The time came when Jesus had to leave—when God called his family to return to the promised land so their child could fulfill his destiny.

Interestingly, God didn't clear up all the risks before he "called his Son out of Egypt." Israel still wasn't a safe place for the infant Jesus. But it seems God saw another, greater danger in remaining outside the promised land.

Earlier I said that Egypt represents many things in Old Testament typology. First, slavery. Second, lesser revelation. But after the exodus took place, Egypt began to represent something else: the temptation to flee the dangers that come with God's calling and return to a place of apparent safety. Egypt represents the idolatry of looking to human powers to be our refuge instead of looking to God. It represents the temptation to go back on our commitment to God and trade our freedom for the apparent safety of slavery.

In our own lives, we often take up temporary refuge in places where God sets us. But the time comes when we have to leave that shelter and step out into the riskier, more dangerous world where our destiny awaits.

If we don't—if we try to cling to our temporary refuge as though it is our eternal home—we will end up in slavery again.

Egypt serves its purpose for a time. But when God calls us out, we have to answer.

What awaits us beyond the borders of Egypt is greater freedom and greater revelation—a knowledge of God and relationship with him that will supersede anything we have known before. Stepping away from our place of safety is risky. But the greater risk is staying, and failing to see the greatness and love of the God who is calling us out.

Being warned in a dream, [Joseph] withdrew to the region of Galilee. Then he went and settled in a town called Nazareth to fulfill what was spoken through the prophets, that He will be called a Nazarene.
(Matthew 2:23)

7

Following the Nazarene: Puns, Holiness, and How to Become a Saint

If it was odd for Matthew to apply Hosea 11:1 ("Out of Egypt I called my Son") to Jesus, the claim he makes here is far odder. As we saw in the last chapter, Hosea 11:1 is arguably not a prophecy—but the prophecy cited here, "He will be called a Nazarene," does not even exist. There is no such statement anywhere in the Old Testament.

This explains an apparent contradiction in the gospels. In John 7:52, the Pharisees were able to call Jesus's identity as the Messiah into question on the basis of his being from Nazareth, a town in Galilee: "Search and look," they said; "No prophet arises from Galilee." Obviously, this wouldn't make any sense if the Old Testament had laid down a clear expectation of a Nazarene Messiah.

But we've already learned that the prophecies

of Matthew are not just straight predictive statements: they include typology. And in this case, they include puns.

God plays with words. That shouldn't surprise us, maybe, given that he created the whole world with them. Wordplay occurs surprisingly often throughout the Bible, and often it originates with God. This appears to be one of those occasions.

Finding the Old Testament "Nazarene"

The town of Nazareth is never mentioned in the Old Testament, so "Nazarenes" as such do not exist in the Old Testament world. The word does sound, however, a lot like "Nazirite."

In Numbers 6, we read about Nazirite vows and the people who took them, who were called Nazirites. A Nazirite vow set the vowed individual apart for a time—in a few rare cases, a lifetime—during which he or she was under strict restrictions. A Nazirite was forbidden to touch anything dead or otherwise become ceremonially unclean, even under extreme circumstances like a death in the family. Nazirites could not cut their hair or drink wine. The Bible's most famous Nazirite is Samson, who blew off all the vows imposed on him at birth, but there are others—Samuel, and almost certainly John the Baptist. The vow Paul took in Acts 18 was likely a temporary Nazirite vow.

Jesus, on the other hand, wasn't a Nazirite as far as we can tell.[1] He drank wine and touched dead and unclean people. Of course, when he did, they miraculously became alive and/or clean—but that doesn't negate the fact that he doesn't seem to have been under a holy vow not to touch them in the first place.

The pun—and I believe the key to this statement of Matthew's—lies in the Hebrew root of the word Nazirite, *nazir,* which is a close soundalike to the root word for the town name Nazareth *(nasar)* and by extension the designation Nazarene. *Nazir* means to consecrate or separate. As Numbers 6:8 puts it: "All the days of his separation he is holy to the LORD."

Here, the description fits well indeed. From the very beginning, Jesus was consecrated to the service of God. As a twelve-year-old boy he was found in the temple, busy "about my Father's business." He was not merely *a* "consecrated one" but *the* Consecrated One—a man separated from the world even as he lived within it, served within it, and carried out his relationship with God within it. And of course, the entire Old Testament indicates that it should be so. In this sense, Matthew is absolutely right: all the prophets knew that the Messiah would be called "separated unto God."

---

1   It is possible that Jesus's declaration at the Last Supper, that he would not drink wine again until he drank it new in the Father's kingdom, is meant to signal a Nazirite vow—a special consecration just before his crucifixion.

In the World but Not of It

It's interesting that early followers of Jesus were called Nazarenes (and even today, in the Middle East, the designation continues). Like Jesus, we are separated ones, consecrated people, holy to the LORD. In fact, this idea of being separated for the Lord lies at the center of New Testament teaching about the church. The passage below uses the word "sanctify" in English. I have replaced this with its literal meaning, which is "set apart":

> I have given them your word, and the world has hated them because they are not of the world, just as I am not of the world. I do not ask that you take them out of the world, but that you keep them from the evil one. They are not of the world, just as I am not of the world. [Set them apart] in the truth; your word is truth. As you sent me into the world, so I have sent them into the world. And for their sake I [set myself apart], that they also may be [set apart] in truth. (John 17:14–19, ESV)

"In the world but not of it" may be one of the most misused phrases in the Bible. Jesus's separation from the world never meant isolating himself or creating a new "holiness code" for dress or other externals. Instead, Jesus knew that being set apart from the world was a matter of living in wholehearted relationship with God, doing his work and worshiping him in Spirit and in Truth. It was about consecration: being dedicated to God as sacred.

Jesus knew too that the only way to save the world is to separate from it. That's a principle seen throughout human society. Think of a Marine, who separates himself from civilians in order to defend them; or even of a politician or celebrity, who at once represents the people and is not one of them. Leadership by its very nature separates. Serving and saving separate. Relationship with God separates.

Like Jesus, we are called holy ones—the literal meaning of "saints," the New Testament's favorite word for the people of God. We are in the world, but not of the world. At the same time, we are here not to condemn but to save—not to isolate ourselves from the rest of humanity, but to consecrate ourselves to the service of God as he serves that same humanity in mercy and truth.

If we want power to change our world, we'll find it in consecration to God. We'll find it by becoming Nazarenes and following the Nazarene.

Interestingly, one theory claims that the word at the root of *Nazarene* is the Aramaic *nasar,* meaning "watchtower."[2] As consecrated servants of God, we are empowered to watch—to guard, to protect, and to herald the coming of the kingdom of God, even as Jesus did. In our consecration is a place of safety for the world.

---

[2] Geoffrey W. Bromiley, ed., "Nazareth," The International Standard Bible Encyclopedia (Grand Rapids: Wm. B. Eerdmans, 1979)

"Repent," John the Baptist cried in the desert, "for the kingdom of heaven is at hand!"

(Matthew 3:3, ESV)

8

The Kingdom at Hand: The Gospel Is Bigger Than You Think

The words "at hand" are meant metaphorically; they indicate something so close it is at our fingertips. John is not foretelling something to come but something that has arrived. The kingdom has come. It is no longer far off, it is no longer future. It is at hand—reachable, touchable, present.

Jesus, Matthew tells us, preached the same thing. Repent, for the kingdom of heaven has come near. The Bible calls this "the gospel"—the good news—"of the kingdom."

In our day "the gospel" has become this very narrow, very personal thing: the gospel is that Jesus died for our sins so we can be forgiven and go to heaven when we die.

But the biblical gospel is the gospel of the kingdom.

It's individual, yes. It's personal, yes. The invitation to enter the kingdom is an invitation to be born again. It does not get more individual, more personal, than that.

But it doesn't end there. This is a kingdom that sets up shop in the hearts of men and women, reigns there, and spills over into the world like yeast in a batch of bread dough. It starts as the tiniest of seeds but eventually becomes a great tree, giving shelter and refuge to all. It starts as a handful of fishermen following a wandering rabbi and ends as a city descending from heaven to earth and filling the world with its light.

The Gospel That's Bigger than We Are

Ultimately, that's why the kingdom of God is worth our passion and commitment. Because it isn't just about us. We need something bigger than ourselves, bigger than our own comfort, in order to find real happiness and fulfillment in life. The God in whose image we are created is always doing things with mutual glory in mind: he glorifies himself, he glorifies us, he glorifies creation (see Romans 8:17–21). He's all about magnification and multiplication and blessing. He's all about doing things that spread out beyond himself and impact others. We are wired to function the same way.

The kingdom is not just about you getting a

ticket to heaven. It's not even just about you and your relationship with God. It's about all of creation coming under the lordship of the Blessed King. It's about the world being anointed with the glory and goodness of God until our cup runs over. It's about good triumphing over evil—in your heart, in my heart, in your life, in my life, in our society, in our descendants, *ad infinitum*.

In those days John the Baptist came preaching in the wilderness of Judea, "Repent, for the kingdom of heaven is at hand."

(Matthew 3:1–2, ESV)

9

To Repent Is to Hope: The Invitation of John's Call to Repentance

To many of us I think the word "repent" conjures up visions of angry fundamentalists picketing funerals or rock concerts, or maybe of old-school preachers raining down fire and brimstone every Sunday morning to people who are supposedly already in a right relationship with God. (No, I don't really understand why that's a thing.)

The call to repentance in Matthew is very different. Although John did warn his hearers of coming judgment, the call for repentance is the polar opposite of doom and gloom. It's light breaking out over a dark horizon, announcing that the day has come. It's hope.

Whenever there's a sudden change of kingship in the world—not the kind that comes because an old king dies and his heir takes the throne, but the kind that comes from a radical revolution or a coup or a conquering of one nation by another, all of which is the kind that Jesus's coming was—it's very good news for some people and very bad news for others.

Good news for those who supported and allied with the new king.

Bad news for those who opposed him.

That's why John's call to repentance has such an urgent, warning tone to it: A new king is here. The old one has been ousted. If you're on the wrong side, you're in trouble.

But that's where it gets beautiful. Because he didn't come crying "Flee!" He didn't come crying, "Never dare show your face here again."

He came crying "Repent."

The word means change your mind. It means *turn*.

Turn around. Go the other way. It implies a new way is possible. It suggests we can change.

In this case, the call to repent—not merely cower, plead, or run for your life—means the new king wants peace. He wants reconciliation. He wants *you*.

Far more than he wants to judge you, he wants to bring you into his kingdom as a friend.

> And Jesus said to him, "Today salvation has come to this house, since he also is a son of Abraham. For the Son of Man came to seek and to save the lost." (Luke 19:9–10, ESV)

Repent is the sound of Love calling out to the broken and huddled in shadows, lonely for home and fearful of ever facing the Father again: "Come home, it's okay, we can be whole again."

Repent means there is hope when we thought all hope was lost.

Repent means the new regime is good and gracious toward you, and you're invited into the new power, the new wealth, the new freedom, the new day.

Repent is a second chance. It is the sweet sound of chains falling away.

There are no limits. The call went out to sinners and saints, seekers and hypocrites, Romans and Jews, prostitutes and Pharisees and disciples.

The kingdom of heaven is at hand. It's here. It's as close as your fingertips. The king has come. The takeover has happened.

So repent.

Do it today.

If you are walking away from God, turn around.

If you are caught in sin, call out for freedom.

If you are stuck in bitterness and darkness and selfishness and pride, change.

You can.

You're allowed.

You're *welcome.*

That's what "repent" means.

In my own life, I have experienced the beauty of repentance when, at various points, God has course-corrected my heart or actions. He rebukes, and there's always a little sting in it, but with his rebuke comes the incredible freedom of clarity and the power to take a different path.

Let me say that again:

Repentance is the power to take a different path.

Isn't that, more than anything, what we need?

Lost and lonely, beaten and broken, estranged and at enmity, dehumanized, deformed, defiled. Going the wrong way and feeling powerless to stop ourselves. We can change. We can walk a different road. We can go home.

Back in Matthew 1:21, an angel told Joseph to name Mary's son Jesus, "for he will save his people from their sins."

Repent. For the kingdom of heaven is at hand.

In those days John the Baptist came preaching in the wilderness of Judea, "Repent, for the kingdom of heaven is at hand." For this is he who was spoken of by the prophet Isaiah when he said, *"The voice of one crying in the wilderness: 'Prepare the way of the Lord; make his paths straight.'"*

(Matthew 1:1–3, ESV)

10

Make His Paths Straight: Getting Our Hearts Ready for the King

The word translated "straight" can also read "level," a rendering that gives us a better picture of John the Baptist's role. In the ancient world, roads were not paved as they are now, and even the best of them would quickly become damaged by rain, by flooding, by heat, by the constant treading of camels and cattle and people and armies and whatever else. The way into a city would be marred, rough, uneven.

When a significant individual was due to come for a visit, then—say a king or a conquering general—a herald would be sent out to announce his coming and galvanize the people into, literally, preparing the way. They would level raised places and raise up collapsed areas. They would clear boulders and debris and fill in holes. All of their efforts were to create a smoother, straighter path.

This is the action seen in Jesus's triumphal entry into Jerusalem later in his life, when palm branches and coats were laid in the street before him to create a clean, level way into the city. As they shouted "Hosanna to the Son of David!", they were consciously welcoming a king.

In describing John the Baptist, Matthew is quoting Isaiah 40:3–5. Isaiah gives us a fuller picture of the scope of the preparation needed:

> A voice cries:
> "In the wilderness prepare the way of the LORD;
> make straight in the desert a highway for our God.
> Every valley shall be lifted up,
> and every mountain and hill be made low;
> the uneven ground shall become level,
> and the rough places a plain.
>
> "And the glory of the LORD shall be revealed,
> and all flesh shall see it together,
> for the mouth of the LORD has spoken."

Making Jesus's paths straight was not a simple matter of filling in a few potholes and smoothing out a few gravel piles. It was a matter of lifting up entire valleys, lowering whole mountains. For this wasn't just any king coming behind John: it was the

Lord Yahweh in the flesh. This highway was not prepared simply for an earthly heir to David's dynasty but for our very God.

Isaiah's image of preparing a way is not literal but figurative. It speaks of "leveling the playing field" in a sense, doing away with the distinctions of power and wealth and poverty and oppression. It speaks of the Great Reversal that Jesus came to bring.

> Go on up to a high mountain,
> O Zion, herald of good news;
> lift up your voice with strength,
> O Jerusalem, herald of good news;
> lift it up, fear not;
> say to the cities of Judah,
> "Behold your God!"
> (Isaiah 40:9)

With John's infamous cry to "Repent, for the kingdom of heaven is at hand," Isaiah's prophecy takes on an urgent personal note. As the disciples discovered, Jesus's intention was not to manifest and enforce his kingship politically or geographically right off the bat. Instead, the cry becomes to prepare the way in our hearts, in our lives.

Make low the pride that stands in our way.

Lift up the love and faith that have lain dormant in our hearts.

Reach out to our fellow human beings with humility and honor. Do away with the distinctions that divide us.

Smooth out the rough places where God has not been welcome.

Level the uneven ground.

Do whatever it takes to be ready for him.

The One who is coming, who is here, who is ready to reveal his glory and come through the gates of our lives, is the Ancient of Days, the Mighty God of old.

> Lift up your heads, O gates!
> And be lifted up, O ancient doors,
> that the King of glory may come in.
> Who is this King of glory?
> The LORD, strong and mighty,
> the LORD, mighty in battle!
> Lift up your heads, O gates!
> And lift them up, O ancient doors,
> that the King of glory may come in.
> Who is this King of glory?
> The LORD of hosts,
> he is the King of glory! Selah.
> (Psalm 24:7–10, ESV)

> For this is he that was spoken of by the prophet Esaias, saying, The voice of one crying in the wilderness, Prepare ye the way of the Lord, make his paths straight.
>
> (Matthew 3:3, KJV)

11

Preparing the Way: Why "Reconcile" Must Be the Chief Cry of Our Hearts

> Therefore, we are ambassadors for Christ, certain that God is appealing through us. We plead on Christ's behalf, "Be reconciled to God." (2 Corinthians 5:20)

Although the call to repent implies sin and judgment (there must be something to "repent" from), we have seen in the last three chapters that John's cry for repentance is not in itself a statement of condemnation so much as it is an offer of hope: it is an invitation to change, to be reconciled with the King.

John's cry *("Prepare the way; make his paths straight!")* was pertinent in his day, with Jesus about to be revealed as Israel's Messiah, but it continues to be pertinent in ours—in our in-between era, wherein the kingdom has already come but is not fully here yet; in which the period of repentance, the period of open invitation and invited response, is extended. In fact it is God's desire that all the world answer this invitation that delays Jesus's return.

> The Lord does not delay His promise, as some understand delay, but is patient with you, not wanting any to perish but all to come to repentance. (2 Peter 3:9)

This period of apparent delay calls forth as many reactions from Christians as there are shades of Christian. Some act like he won't return at all. Others embrace a kind of news-watching, Revelation-cherry-picking doom-and-gloomism. Still others are actively trying to act as modern John the Baptists, getting our generation ready for a return of Christ that may be right around the corner; while still others wait for his return in more mundane (but no less real) ways. We treat the concept of Christ's return with varying levels of guilt, panic, indifference, confusion, fear, happiness, escapism, and real joy.

But Paul tells us what we should do during this time: we should share in God's heart and plead, like Paul did, "Be reconciled to God."

There is still time. As long as this present world remains, there is still hope for those around us—

our friends, our families, our neighbors, the nations. And that's the point, isn't it? Peter says the Lord is waiting not because he's cooking up a really nasty judgment day but because he loves everyone and wants them to repent. Time and God's kindness will, apparently, allow for a lot more repentance before Jesus returns.

Recall the imagery in Isaiah and Matthew of preparing the way for the Lord. This is our task and our opportunity. Prepare the way. Clear the road. Level and smooth out the rough and broken places. Lay our own lives down on the road like palm branches and like coats, preparing for the final and glorious triumphal entry.

What does that look like—practically? What does it look like to prepare the way for Christ in our own lifestyles, our own spirits, our own day-by-day existence? What does it look like to prepare the way for him in the church? (Don't look now, but I suspect our road is full of potholes, boulders, and broken asphalt. Time to level things out again!)

Going even further—what about preparing the way for Jesus in society? Is that possible? What does that even look like? I don't know, but if every action and word we speak as representatives of Christ in this world doesn't send back the echo "Be reconciled to God!", then I think we're doing it wrong. I don't mean doing street-corner evangelism every day. I mean living our lives in a way that invites and attracts people to be reconciled to the Father who loves them and who is waiting for them to come home.

Things are bad in our society and culture right now; it's true. Things are rocky all around the world. But I hope that instead of looking at the mess, reading some scintillating prophecy book, and declaring that God's clearly getting ready to torch the whole road, we will consider rolling up our sleeves, whistling while we work, and preparing the way.

Joyfully, with anticipation. With singing.

Our King is coming, after all.

But when he saw many of the Pharisees and Sadducees coming to where he was baptizing, he said to them: "You brood of vipers! Who warned you to flee from the coming wrath? Produce fruit in keeping with repentance. And do not think you can say to yourselves, 'We have Abraham as our father.' I tell you that out of these stones God can raise up children for Abraham. The ax is already at the root of the trees, and every tree that does not produce good fruit will be cut down and thrown into the fire."

(Matthew 3:7–10, NIV)

12

Getting Real About Wrath: An Invitation From a (Justifiably) Angry God

By this time, we've looked deeply at the cry of John the Baptist, "Repent, for the kingdom of heaven is at hand!" as an invitation from a loving God. We have seen the kingdom as opportunity, as transformative power on the inside of our society and our world and our souls. Really, the whole Bible is an invitation. Invitation to engage, to relate, to wrestle, to change. To step into the presence of a Holy God and not die because astonishingly, he has given us his life.

The Bible itself is not our ultimate reality or end game; everything in it invites us into an experience of the Truth who is God.

But on the other side of the invitation is sober warning. Why wouldn't that be true? We live in a world that is cursed. We ourselves are cursed. This is self-evident. We don't need the Bible to tell us we have problems even though we want to be better, or that we're all dying even though something inside all of us wants to last.

John the Baptist's warnings pull no punches (and contain no tact): *"You brood of vipers! Who warned you to flee from the wrath to come?"*

Wrath is not a popular topic these days, but I'm glad God is angry.

I couldn't respect a God who wasn't. Could you? People starve to death in our world because other people are greedy and dishonest. People molest and abuse and murder; people prostitute and manipulate and use one another. Political power and money and personal autonomy are idolized by millions and leave millions more broken behind them.

Yes, God is angry. So will you be, if you spend even a few raw minutes thinking deeply about the situations of which he is constantly, fully aware.

Choosing Sides and Bearing Fruit

As respected and visibly pious religious and political leaders, the Pharisees and Sadducees—one a powerful religious faction and the other more of an aristocratic elite—didn't expect to get singled out as a brood of vipers when they showed up to oversee the rabble-rousing dunker from the desert.

We saw a few chapters back that when a new king comes, people divide into two groups: one happy, one not so much. These groups are "those who supported the new king before he rose to power" and "those who didn't."

New kings in the ancient world usually made pretty quick work of the enemy in the land. If you'd shown yourself to be on the wrong side before the throne changed hands, at best you'd lose your position of power and probably your home and possessions. At worst you'd lose your head.

The coming of the kingdom of heaven is good news for whole nations of people, but there is also wrath to come. It all depends on how we respond to the King who comes—which side we choose to take.

> I baptize you with water for repentance. But after me comes one who is more powerful than I, whose sandals I am not worthy to carry. He will baptize you with the Holy Spirit and fire. His winnowing fork is in his hand, and he will clear his threshing floor, gathering his wheat into the barn and burning up the chaff with unquenchable fire. (Matthew 3:11–12, NIV)

John's word pictures of trees and wheat remind us that we are not here just to take up space. Humanity was always meant to be fully alive and to give life. We were meant to be recipients and conduits of blessing and to manifest the life of the Vine in the world.[1] A fruit tree that never bears fruit is not what it's supposed to be. When wheat is threshed, wind blows away the lifeless chaff and leaves the heavier grain of wheat—a seed full of life, one small thing with a harvest locked inside it—behind.

If we fail to bear fruit, we are worthy of judgment. We have not done what we were designed, equipped, and given the responsibility to do. We have in fact done the opposite. And we are able to bear fruit only by remaining in the Vine—by choosing relationship with the King.

In Moses's day God said, "I have set before you life and death, blessing and curse. Choose life" (Deuteronomy 30:19).

The same call stands today. We too are given the opportunity to choose. To take sides in this era of changing thrones and shifting kingdoms. It is clear whose the final victory will be. It is clear who will ultimately put his enemies under his feet.

But if we find that our autonomy, our status, our self-righteousness is too threatened by the new King, we will reject him—as the Pharisees and Sadducees did.

If we are too committed to the emptiness of

---

[1] John 15:4–6, 16

hypocrisy and the tyranny of this present age to give it up and exchange it for authenticity and eternal life, we will find ourselves blowing away with the chaff.

John told the Pharisees and Sadducees not to take refuge in their ancestry. We, too, find a lot of things to take refuge in. A lot of ways to assure ourselves we'll be fine, even if we stay committed to the old regime. A lot of ways to excuse lifelessness and unfaithfulness.

They won't cut it.

If we do not abandon our excuses and run into the kingdom of life, we, who got suckered in by the fruit of the tree of the knowledge of good and evil, will stand on the landscape of the earth as a dead, rotted-out, finally barren tree.

But it's not too late to choose life.

It's not too late to repent.

Then Jesus came from Galilee to John at the Jordan, to be baptized by him. But John tried to stop Him, saying, "I need to be baptized by You, and yet You come to me?" Jesus answered him, "Allow it for now, because this is the way for us to fulfill all righteousness." Then he allowed Him to be baptized. After Jesus was baptized, He went up immediately from the water. The heavens suddenly opened for Him, and He saw the Spirit of God descending like a dove and coming down on Him. And there came a voice from heaven: "This is My beloved Son. I take delight in Him!"

(Matthew 3:13–17)

13

Out of the Water: How History Culminates in Jesus's Baptism

This—the beginning of Jesus's public ministry. This—one of the most beautiful moments in the New Testament.

Beautiful, moving, and mysterious.

What is *happening* here? Have you ever wondered that?

When Jesus came to him and asked to be baptized, John almost refused. He wanted to be baptized by Jesus instead.

But Jesus, he was committed to going all the way with us.

"Let's do this thing," he told John; "it's the way we will fulfill all righteousness."

The Vulnerable Son

One of my favorite things in this whole image is how it shines light on Jesus's own vulnerability and need to be loved and approved. In the very moment he begins his incredibly difficult ministry, a three-year journey that he knows will lead to his death, he is both physically touched and verbally (and publicly) affirmed as God's Son.

"I take delight in him!"

Or as other translations say: *"In him I am well-pleased!"*

Fulfill All Righteousness?

But I got thinking about that word "fulfill" and the way it points to the culmination of something.

"Fulfill" is a prophecy word, not an obedience word. When we drive like we're supposed to, we don't say we fulfilled the speed limit.

In Greek it means to fill or complete. Nearly every use in Matthew is connected to the fulfillment of Old Testament prophecy.[1] From moment one, Matthew's story has been replete with types and shadows, showing Jesus everywhere in the Old Testament. We have seen Jesus in Abraham, in David, in Israel leaving Egypt, in the consecration of the Nazirites. And the Old Testament is full of water pictures.

---

[1] There are three (possible) exceptions. Once it refers to Jesus coming to "fulfill" the law—but this is arguably also a matter of prophecy, speaking of Jesus fulfilling the types and shadows found in the law rather than necessarily obeying every point of it (though he did that too). Once it refers to filling a fishing net; and once Jesus tells the religious leaders to "fill up the measure of their fathers" by killing him as their forefathers killed the prophets.

So he's there too.

He's in the Levitical priests washing to be clean for their ritual service.

He's in Naaman the leper going into the water diseased and dying and coming up cleansed and newly alive.

He's in Moses (of course) drawn out of the water as a child—the promised Deliverer come at last and rescued from death by a basket and a river.

And he's in Noah.

Suddenly I understood the dove.

The Sign of New Creation

Millennia ago, the only survivor of an old world sent out a dove to see if the new world had come up from the waters of judgment. It went out and brought back an olive branch—a sign of new life budding somewhere after so much desolation.

A sign that hope had risen from the water, that it was not over after all.

The second time Noah sent out a dove, it never came back.

And thousands of years later, a man rose out of the water with a new world, a new humanity, a new life inside of him . . . and a dove came from the sky to greet him.

To find rest at last in the new world born out of the old one.

The Spirit of God, wandering for thousands of years, at long last come home to touch humanity and remain. In this moment, Jesus opened a new story. At this moment, a new creation could be discerned on the horizon of an old and flooded world. He had come to "fulfill all righteousness"—to finish all the stories and set the whole of creation to rights again.

Therefore, if anyone is in the Messiah, he is a new creation. Old things have disappeared, and—look!—all things have become new! (2 Corinthians 5:17, ISV)

Then Jesus was led up by the Spirit into the wilderness to be tempted by the devil. After He had fasted forty days and forty nights, He was hungry. Then the tempter approached Him and said, 'If you are the Son of God, tell these stones to become bread."

(Matthew 4:1–3)

14

"If You Are": What the Temptation of Jesus Reveals About Our Deadliest Trap

For years I read the story of Jesus's temptation in the wilderness and thought, "Say what?" I couldn't understand what in the world these temptations were about, much less how they related to human experience (i.e. my experience).

Turning stones into bread wouldn't even be a sin. I have never been tempted to throw myself off a building. You see what I mean.

All I managed to take away from this strange little interlude was that Jesus was apparently nothing like me, and Satan's skills at tempting were a lot less impressive than they're cracked up to be.

But then I saw it.

Three words at the base of every temptation that turned Satan's strangely baited lures into deadly traps . . . and shed incredible light on our own lives, on what means most to us, on our deepest needs, our deadliest temptation, and what stops many of us from making any real progress in our spiritual lives.

Because many of us have already taken the bait.

Prove It

The best traps don't come to us declaring, "I'm a trap!" They hide their triggers. Disguise themselves. In this case the trigger is hidden in three little words.

"If you are."

Satan wasn't trying to get Jesus to do things that would be wrong in and of themselves. Presumably he knew better than to try to tempt Jesus with destructive, ugly actions that would have been repugnant to him.

Instead, he called Jesus's identity into question.

He invited Jesus to doubt.

"If you are the Son of God . . . turn these stones into bread."

"If you are the Son of God . . . throw yourself down from the temple."

"If you are the one destined to rule the world, bow down and worship me and I'll give you what you want."

If you are.

Remember, immediately prior to Jesus's entry to the wilderness, he was baptized, and a voice from heaven thundered, "This is my beloved Son."

Now, forty days later, when Jesus was physically weak and exhausted, Satan showed up to lay a trap he has laid hundreds of thousands of times throughout history. Almost certainly, he's laid it for you.

If you are.

If God loves you.

If you are his child.

Prove it.

Show me.

The Trajectory of Temptation

Satan has been calling God's words into question since the garden. That was the shape of the first temptation: "Did God really say that? Does he really mean it? Test him. He's holding out on you."

This is why it's so significant that in every case, Jesus quoted Scripture back to Satan. In essence, he said, "I don't have to prove anything to you. What God says is true, and I believe it."

Jesus refused to enter into the conversation Satan was trying to start. He understood that temptation has a trajectory. The enemy is trying to lead us down a path that won't end with the first question.

For me, understanding of this story came when I asked "what if."

What if Jesus had tried to turn the stones into bread, and God hadn't empowered him to do it?

What if, for whatever reason, the power of the Spirit hadn't been present for that task?

Here it is, my friends, the snare:

If Jesus had hinged his identity, his belief that he was who God said he was, on an outcome in his circumstances, then not getting that outcome would have had the potential to destroy his identity.

And with it, the trust on which his entire relationship with the Father was built.

The Temptation to Doubt

How often have you heard the echoes of exactly this decision before?

I used to believe in God, but my mother died even though I prayed that she wouldn't. So now I'm an atheist.

I grew up in church, but God let my parents divorce, so I don't go anymore.

I asked God to heal my marriage, but my husband left. If God loves me, why would he allow that to happen?

Like us, Jesus was born into a fallen world, and

he was subject to the kinds of doubt endemic to such a world, just as we are. Here's the thing: suffering is a reality in a broken world. People make choices. Things happen that we can't understand. The fact is we are finite, and we do not always pray in accordance with God's will because we don't have the perspective to do so. If, in the midst of that, we choose to hold our belief in God's love for us hostage to particular outcomes, we will end up ensnared.

And the worst thing is, the trap doesn't end. Remember, temptation has a trajectory. Hinging our belief in God on particular outcomes in this world leads to a lifelong spiral of doubt. It does so for us, and it would have done so for Jesus if he had taken the bait.

Once you've started calling God's word into doubt, once you've started hinging your belief in his love on particular answers or outcomes, you will have to do it again. Your trust will become so tied to your circumstances that every time something does not go well, God's love will be up for question again.

Jesus refused to play the game.

He just refused to step into the snare.

He didn't even address the root temptation to question his identity. He ignored it. That's how little he was willing to let Satan plant the seeds of doubt in his relationship to his Father.

Satan went after Jesus's identity in the three key areas of provision, protection, and purpose, and every time, Jesus refused to play.

It's Time to Set Yourself Free

This story, once so puzzling to me, now strikes me as profound—and profoundly personal. I hear, much more clearly, the voice in my life whispering, "If you are." I'm able to do what Jesus did and refuse to play the game. I'm empowered to stand on the Word of God.

But I'm also challenged and offered freedom, because somewhere in the past, I've bought the temptation before. I have hinged my belief in God's love on outcomes, on circumstances, on certain factors in life coming to pass. And I have been thrown into doubt and even despair when things didn't pan out.

If you're looking down right now and finding there's a snare wire around your ankle, today is the day to set yourself free.

Recognize that God does love you. You are his child. His word says so. His sacrifice proves it. You can't understand all the mysteries of life and its circumstances right now. But you can trust the Father and be free.

At the end of the story in Matthew 4, we're told "Then the Devil left him, and immediately angels came and began to serve Him" (Matthew 4:11). Of course, the enemy would be back. But in the meantime, God had always had Jesus's needs in mind. He was in fact ready to step in and feed him in his moment of hunger. But even if he hadn't, if Jesus had gone on being hungry, it wouldn't have changed a thing. He would still have been seen, known, and loved, and the Father's ultimate intentions for him would have been unmoved. The only thing needed to allow Jesus to access the Father was trust—and it was trust he was willing to give unconditionally.

When He heard that John had been arrested, He withdrew into Galilee. He left Nazareth behind and went to live in Capernaum by the sea, in the region of Zebulun and Naphtali.

(Matthew 4:12–13)

15

What Faith Really Means: Ordinary Trust and That Time Jesus Moved Away from Home

It's easy to think of the life of Jesus as one long list of supernatural extravagances: *Be born of a virgin, check. Be baptized during a heavenly visitation, check. Go toe-to-toe with Satan, check. And then it's ministry, miracles, save the whole world, check.*

Oh, and that time Jesus moved away from home.

You know, that time when things were getting kind of hot for the guys in his social circle, so he moved out of his parents' place to go up north a bit and start over somewhere else.

You didn't know about that?

In Matthew 4:12–13, Jesus left Nazareth behind and moved a little deeper in Galilee, going to live in Capernaum. He was thirty years old. His cousin and presumably friend, John ("the Baptizer"), had just been arrested for stirring up the same kind of trouble Jesus tended to stir up, and when Jesus heard about it, he moved away.

An Ordinary Event...

Why exactly did he choose to leave Nazareth? Matthew doesn't say. Maybe it was safer in Capernaum. Maybe he wanted to get away from his old surroundings and clear his head. Maybe, on the cusp of beginning his ministry, he just wanted his home base to feel new.

What strikes me about this story is how *ordinary* it is. Jesus, moving away from home at age thirty. Jesus, responding to circumstances. Jesus, having a social circle that influenced him.

Jesus, living life like we do.

...With Extraordinary Purpose

And yet Matthew mentions that Capernaum was located in the ancient tribal lands of Naphtali, and he comments on Jesus's move with a passage from Isaiah, written seven hundred or so years earlier:

> The land of Zebulun and the land of Naphtali,
> > the way of the sea, beyond the Jordan,

> Galilee of the Gentiles
> the people dwelling in darkness
>> have seen a great light,
> and for those dwelling in the region and shadow of death,
>> on them a light has dawned.
> (Matthew 4:15–16, ESV)

In a pattern that should be familiar to us by now, Matthew sees the fulfillment of prophecy even in this immensely ordinary event. In Jesus's moving out, he sees the epic story of light breaking into darkness. He sees the glory of God breaking into thick gloom and despair, transforming it.

Jesus moved out of his parents' house, for apparently circumstantial reasons and not in response to a heavenly order or angelic visit. It was such an ordinary thing to do. Yet God worked his extraordinary purpose through it.

What It Really Means to Live by Faith

Living in this world as Christians—Christians who are eager to live out our purpose, to follow God, to know Christ to the fullest and be led by the Spirit in all we do—it's easy to feel like, if we do anything just because it makes sense with our circumstances, we're failing God somehow. I mean, anybody can move out just because it seems like the right thing to do. Surely a really spiritual, obedient, Spirit-filled believer would wait for orders from heaven.

Surely Christians are supposed to float over the realities of the world, looking down on the grit and the confusion and the . . . well, the humanness . . . in favor of a transcendent, supernatural existence.

Surely we should always know what's really going on and should act with clear purpose at all times.

Surely that's what a life of faith *means*.

I remember when it first hit me that a life of faith actually meant acting, at times, without a clear reason or understanding. Sometimes it meant doing what had to be done and trusting that God was working through it somehow.

A life with God does not always look like a blazing path laid out before us: often it looks like one step after another, with just enough light to see where to put a foot down.

And sometimes not even that.

God's Hidden Purpose

While I am not very okay with this reality, it seems that God is. In fact, it seems he has designed faith to work this way. Occasionally I act with understanding. Much of the time I feel like I'm fumbling in the dark. But God does not want my faith to be in my understanding, my spirituality, or my "clear leading of the Holy Spirit." He wants it to be in *him*, period.

Which means that even when I don't know why certain things are happening, or why I feel pushed to make a certain decision, I can trust that he has some hidden purpose behind it.

I can trust that because he is in me always, and because it's by the blood of Christ that I'm accepted and right with him, I can know that even when I can't see answers, he's at work.

I might feel like I'm just moving across town. *He* knows he's shining a light through thick darkness or fulfilling a purpose he's had in waiting for seven hundred years.

I might feel like I'm running scared because something has happened in my social circles that's got me rattled. *He* knows he's positioning me for greater impact.

I might feel like I just need to clear my head.

He knows the revelation he has in store, just around the next bend.

The Context of the Ordinary

The truth is we all live ordinary lives, and everything supernatural, unusual, and extraordinary God wants to do through us—and he does want to do such things—will be worked out in the context of ordinary life.

Everything we experience will happen within the context of ordinary circumstances, good and bad. Of human decisions like changing locations, going to school, working a job, getting married. Much of the time the way before us won't be clear. Much of the time we won't understand our road until we're looking back. Hindsight is 20/20. Foresight is usually wrong.

God doesn't ask us to have it all figured out. He asks us to trust.

Maybe that's why Matthew bothers to mention this detail: because Jesus's extraordinary life, which was about to burst onto the stage of Israel in a powerful way, was couched in ordinary trust.

Not a trust that we have it all figured out, but a trust that God does.

From then on Jesus began to preach, "Repent, because the kingdom of heaven has come near!"

(Matthew 4:17)

16

Heaven Is Here:
How the Kingdom of God
Changes Our Questions and Our Lives

If you grew up evangelical, you know that the gospel is this: Jesus died for our sins so we can go to heaven when we die.

The problem is, that's not true. Or rather, it is true, but it's not the gospel—not the whole gospel, not even really the point of the gospel.

The gospel is not ultimately about going to heaven. The gospel is about heaven coming to us.

The gospel has a lot to say about "when we die," but it has just as much (or more) to say about "how we live." The gospel is a total transformation of what it means to live in the first place. After Jesus's baptism, temptation in the wilderness, and move to Capernaum, he began his ministry at last: with the same message John the Baptist had preached.

It was not a message of a far-distant afterlife called "heaven," nor of simply being forgiven for our sins. The message was wider, more encompassing. It was a message of kingdom now.

Repent, for the kingdom of heaven has come near.

The Kingdom of Heaven Has Come Near

With his accounts of Jesus's birth and early life, the coming of John the Baptist, and of Jesus's baptism and temptation, Matthew has set the stage for us to see Jesus not just as an interesting teacher or leader but as the focal point of history, as the fulfillment of thousands of years of prophecy and typology, as God's light breaking into darkness.

It all leads to this moment, to Matthew 4:17.

It all leads to this message: "The kingdom of heaven has come near!"

Jesus's ministry had officially begun. But there's a bigger picture here. Ostensibly, Jesus's ministry lasted three years. Actually, it lasted three years *in Galilee and Judea*. After that, Jesus ascended into the heavens and continued his ministry from the right hand of God.

What Jesus proclaimed in Matthew 4:17 is still true.

The kingdom of heaven has come near.

It is *still* near.

It is still, as some translations have it, "at hand"—within reach, at our fingertips, no longer distant or inaccessible.

A Brief History of the Kingdom of God

Matthew is unique in his use of the term "kingdom of heaven," or more accurately, "kingdom of the heavens." Writing for a Jewish audience, he presumed on their understanding of the term: *heaven* in Old Testament context is not just the distant home of the righteous dead but the invisible, spiritual realm where God is. It coexists with the physical realm and directly impacts it. God's throne exists in the heavens. Angels and even demons also exist in the heavens—in the invisible realm. Heaven is the source of all authority and rule on earth.

Luke, writing to a Gentile audience that may not have understood heaven in the same sense, uses the term "kingdom of God," as do Mark, John, and Paul. The terms are synonymous, because heaven in Jewish understanding was the realm of God.

It's unfortunate that we've grown so used to talking about heaven as a far distant afterlife, a place removed from us. That concept has more in common with pagan notions of a palatial home of the gods, a Mount Olympus where mortals cannot ascend. The Old Testament picture is of a heaven that is immanent: an invisible reality that may be revealed any time God chooses to draw back the curtain and give us a glimpse. The word "heaven" or "heavens" is just as validly (and often) translated "sky." Birds fly in the heavens. Sun, moon, and stars shine in the heavens. Heaven is as immediate as the air we breathe.

We, of course, can't see it. We are physical beings who are, as George Eliot wrote, "well wadded with stupidity." Unless and until God grants us glimpses, we do not see the ocean we swim in.

The Kingdom at War

Historically speaking, we earthlings are also in rebellion against the kingdom of God. God is sovereign, and he rules sovereignly in the invisible realm that lies behind everything we can see and touch. But mankind has been fighting that rule since Eden, as have the whole swath of spiritual beings under Satan's rule.

There is no question of whether or not God reigns. He does. But that doesn't mean everyone is willingly submitted to that rule. In fact, the reality is emphatically the opposite.

This is why the kingdom can be simultaneously here and not here: God reigns, but not everyone bows. Jesus is on the throne now, but he is waiting for his enemies to be made his footstool. We are in the kingdom of heaven now, but we wait for the day when the war will cease and everything will be reconciled in him.

This is a really significant thing to understand, because a sovereign, all-powerful kingdom is a wonderful thing when it's on your side and a terrible thing when it isn't.

Earlier in this book, we were introduced to Jesus as the heir of David. David's kingship was ultimately intended to merge the kingdoms of earth with the kingdom of heaven. Through a man after his own heart, God would rule his people. But David's children rebelled and turned to idols, until God at last cursed his line and left this kingdom of heaven-on-earth with an empty throne.

Jesus came to fill that throne. He came to end the war between God and man and bring the peace—the harmony and wholeness—of reconciliation, extending the direct rule of God to the ends of the earth. Fully human and fully divine, Jesus is God, fulfilling his promise to put David's seed on the throne forever by personally becoming that seed—in the same way that he fulfilled the promise to Abraham to bless the whole world through a child of Abraham by becoming that child.

From then on Jesus began to preach, "Repent, because the kingdom of heaven has come near!"

(Matthew 4:17)

17

The Kingdom at Hand

So what exactly is it that Jesus came preaching? He wasn't creating the kingdom of heaven or setting up the kingdom of God: the kingdom had always existed. Rather, he was bringing the rule of God directly to earth, no longer mediating it through other kings or powers. He was making the throne accessible to us. He was ending the war.

When Jesus said the kingdom had "come near," he meant it in a wondrously literal way: the kingdom of the heavens was walking, visibly, in Galilee: calling disciples, eating and drinking, teaching, preaching, and healing people.

The kingdom had come in the person of one man.

And Jesus showed us what it means to *live* in the kingdom. He showed us what it means to be fully submitted to the rule of God and to have direct access to him. He gave us a picture of the kingdom as a life source.

This is what I meant when I earlier said the gospel is about how we live: not only in the sense of "things we should or shouldn't do," but in the sense of our access, our source, our wellspring, our path—our way of being human and relating to God.

Jesus himself exemplifies the kingdom of heaven. He demonstrates the rule of God in and through a human being, so much so that we might say he is the kingdom of heaven personified. He demonstrates what it means for God to reign directly within a human being, to dwell with his spirit in perfect harmony. Jesus shows us what it means *not* to be at war with God and so to have total access to him, to be under kingdom provision, kingdom law, kingdom goodness, kingdom life. He returns us to the pre-fall world of Genesis, of paradise in Eden, before humanity's trust relationship with God was broken. Eventually Eden will extend all over the earth again, but it begins where the breakdown occurred—in human hearts.

Now and Not Yet

Paul sums up our situation as believers in Colossians 1:13: "He has rescued us from the domain of darkness and transferred us into the kingdom of the Son He loves." The key is has, present tense—

this has already been done. The kingdom of the heavens is here, accessible, at hand. The kingdom of God, as Jesus said in Luke 17:21, is among us.

Yet, the Bible is clear: the kingdom is still coming. Until the whole world is reconciled as we are reconciled, there is a sense in which we still wait, and pray, for "the kingdom come."[1]

In the meantime, we have access to the kingdom through Jesus. "I am the door," he told his disciples in John 10:9. "I am the way, the truth, and the life. No one comes to the Father except through Me."[2]

THE GOSPEL OF THE KINGDOM

The gospel of the kingdom—or, in more modern English, the "good news" of the kingdom[3]—is that the kingdom of God is here, and rather than relating to it as rebels, we are invited to repent and become full citizens. "The kingdom of God," Paul declares in Romans 14:17, is "righteousness, peace, and joy in the Holy Spirit." Hebrews 12:28 declares this "a kingdom that cannot be shaken," in which God's promise to the Son is fulfilled:

---

[1] Matthew 6:10
[2] John 14:6
[3] The word "gospel" derives from Old English "god spel" or "good spell." It literally means "good news." According to Online Etymology Dictionary: "The first element of the Old English word originally had a long 'o,' but it shifted under mistaken association with God, as in 'God-story' (i.e. the history of Christ)." "Good story" thus became "God story" in English—an appropriate transformation indeed.

> Your throne, O God, is forever and ever, and the scepter of Your kingdom is a scepter of justice. (Hebrews 1:8)

We can benefit today from the direct rule of God in our hearts and lives. His righteousness, peace, joy, and justice can be the banner that flies over us. The King has walked among us and opened the door to us all. In fact, that's what it means to be "the church": the Greek word *ekklesia* ("church") means a body of citizens. You haven't been given an entry permit to heaven after you die: you've been given citizenship in heaven here and now.

The invisible kingdom is your kingdom. The invisible realm is the source of your life, and you are in Christ, you are at harmony with it. Its resources, goodness, and power are yours.

If, that is, you have come in through the door and knelt at the throne of the Son of David. If you are in Christ, you are in heaven, and you are a citizen of the kingdom of heaven.

The Questions We Should Ask

I love Matthew so much because it positions Jesus within the big story of creation and redemption: because in Matthew, I come to understand who we are, who Jesus is, and where we're at in history. Understanding those things (as best as I can, anyway!)

leads to a new paradigm that leads to new questions.

If we aren't in fact just waiting to "go to heaven," if we're already in, what does it mean to live in heaven now? ("Don't rejoice that the demons are subject to you," Jesus told his disciples in Luke 10:20; "rejoice that your names are written in heaven").

If Jesus has established the kingdom of heaven on earth and we are full citizens of that kingdom, what is our role in this earth? What are we doing here, actually? (A lot more, I would wager, than "just passing through.")

The gospel of the kingdom changes our questions, and the possible answers, because it offers a very different paradigm than many of us assume.

Jesus's announcement was world-altering in AD 30: "Repent, for the kingdom of heaven *has come near.*" It's still world-altering now.

Jesus didn't immediately vault to an earthly throne and bring the power of the kingdom cracking down dictator style. Instead, he started planting the kingdom in individual human hearts and said it would grow from there.[4] Righteousness, peace, and joy would transform the world from the inside out. The kingdom would be expressed in the obedience of its citizens, who like Jesus would love God and others more than their own lives and would walk in the power of the Holy Spirit.

---

4 Matthew 13:31–33, among others.

We don't just *pray* "your kingdom come," we help answer the prayer.

Heaven is here. It's your kingdom, your home country, your inheritance. How does that change your perspective?

How does it change your *life*?

While walking by the Sea of Galilee, he saw two brothers, Simon (who is called Peter) and Andrew his brother, casting a net into the sea, for they were fishermen. And he said to them, "Follow me, and I will make you fishers of men." Immediately they left their nets and followed him. And going on from there he saw two other brothers, James the son of Zebedee and John his brother, in the boat with Zebedee their father, mending their nets, and he called them. Immediately they left the boat and their father and followed him.

(Matthew 4:18–22)

18

Purpose, Identity, and Why We Can't Start with the Great Commission

In this passage, Matthew tells the story of the day Jesus called his first disciples. It's clear from the other gospels, especially John, that there was more to the story than this. This wasn't a first introduction. Andrew was a disciple of John the Baptist. Peter was Andrew's brother. James and John sometimes partnered with them in business. These young men had already seen Jesus work miracles. And they all lived in Capernaum, where Jesus now lived as well. Jesus took some time to establish his trustworthiness and character with these men before he called them. He spent some time building relationship and getting to know them.

But finally, the day came when it wasn't enough for them just to hang around the edges. Jesus had brought the kingdom of God near, and it was time to start establishing that kingdom on earth in the hearts of other people. Disciples. People who would follow Jesus, learn from him, and spread his teachings and his work.

Starting at the End

When we talk about discipleship, we tend to jump right to the end. Jesus declared he would make these fishermen fishers *of* men, so we immediately recall his last words to them before he ascended to heaven and think of their "discipleship" as a matter of fulfilling those words:

> All authority has been given to Me in heaven and on earth. Go, therefore, and make disciples of all nations, baptizing them in the name of the Father and of the Son and of the Holy Spirit, teaching them to observe everything I have commanded you. And remember, I am with you always, to the end of the age. (Matthew 28:18–20)

In my experience, the responsibility given in this verse is something evangelicals at least are pretty clear on: we are supposed to make disciples. I mean, we are evangelicals. This is what we do! We grasp this fast and easy because it's a task. We can all do tasks. You tell me wash the dishes, I can wash the dishes. But Jesus didn't begin by calling his disciples to a task. He called them to discipleship—to *become* something. I can do a task. But if you tell me "be a doctor," that's a whole different deal. That's eight years of school and knowledge and skills I can't even begin to conceive of now. That's a whole life's work.

The reality is, although I fully support spreading the gospel, we are often guilty of putting the cart before the horse. Because the call of Jesus isn't just to make disciples; it's to *be* one first.

Relationship, Call, and Identity

The Great Commission is not the first thing Jesus said to his disciples. He did not start by giving them a job. He started by calling them into an encounter and relationship with himself.

John 1:38–42 tells us more of the story:

> When Jesus turned and noticed them following Him, He asked them, "What are you looking for?" They said to Him, "Rabbi" (which means "Teacher"), "where are You staying?"
>
> "Come and you'll see," He replied. So they went and saw where He was staying, and they stayed with Him that day. It was about 10 in the morning.

Andrew, Simon Peter's brother, was one of the two who heard John and followed Him. He first found his own brother Simon and told him, "We have found the Messiah!" (which means "Anointed One"), and he brought Simon to Jesus. When Jesus saw him, He said, "You are Simon, son of John. You will be called Cephas" (which means "Rock").

The first thing Jesus said to Peter was, "What are you looking for?" He followed that up with an invitation to know him: "Come and see." He always called people to follow him, to come with him. To Matthew, seated at his table tax collecting, Jesus said, "Get up and come with me."

Second, Jesus cast a vision for them. He told these men what he saw in them, what he would make them. He gave Simon a new name: "You are the rock." Later in the same passage, he promised a disciple named Nathanael that he would see angels ascending and descending on the Son of Man. He didn't tell Andrew, Peter, James, and John, "I will make you catch people." He said, "I will make you fishers of men."

It's an important distinction. Jesus didn't give them a task first. He gave them an identity.

For us, too, discipleship begins here: with an invitation to follow Jesus, to encounter him, to get to know him, to be with him in daily life. In the process of being with Jesus, we learn who we are and what his vision for us is. We learn that he created us and called us for a purpose, and he shapes us in line with that purpose.

Apprentice Children of God

After inviting his disciples into relationship with him and then casting a vision for who they would become, Jesus spent three years teaching them. He was their rabbi, an itinerant teacher. Rabbi and disciple were not foreign roles in their culture any more than professor and student are today, but it was a far more holistic relationship: a disciple didn't just show up for class three times a week. He ate, drank, slept, and breathed the rabbi's teachings and the rabbi's way of life. He followed him everywhere and learned not just what he *said* but what he *did* and how he did it. He was an apprentice of the highest order.

This is often the missing piece in our life as modern Christians. It's not enough to urge one another to share the gospel (though yes, we should do that too). We have to *be* disciples of Jesus before we can make disciples of Jesus.

The disciples were apprentices of Jesus, which means that they were apprentice rabbis. They intended from the start to learn to do what he did—to teach, preach, work miracles, and announce the kingdom of God. But they were far more than that, because Jesus was not just a rabbi: he was a king, and he was the Son of God.

When they wanted to learn to pray, Jesus taught his disciples to begin, "Our Father, who is in heaven." They were not just teachers in training. They were apprentice children of God.[1]

Jesus taught his disciples how to live as God's children. He taught them how to think, how to trust, how to act in alignment with God's will and word. He taught them about the Father's heart for them. He taught them about faith, love, and goodness. He taught them to live fully surrendered to the Father and in a relationship of mutual joy and pleasure with him.

"I Will Make You"

From the start, Jesus made it clear to his disciples that he was giving them a purpose and an identity, and that they would find both in relationship with him. Their job wasn't to make themselves, but to trust in his making of them. All of their work would flow out of that, just as all Jesus's work flowed

---

[1] The concepts of "apprenticing" with Jesus and also the at-handness of the kingdom of God are introduced and explored in Dallas Willard's *The Divine Conspiracy,* a book well worth reading. New York: HarperOne, 1997.

out of his ongoing, daily walk with the Father.

For us, the same promise applies. Jesus, our rabbi, the one who disciples us, has a vision for who we are meant to be and a plan to shape us for that vision. His primary purpose in our lives is to teach us how to live like children of God:

> But to all who did receive him, who believed in his name, he gave the right [power or authority] to become children of God, who were born, not of blood nor of the will of the flesh nor of the will of man, but of God. (John 1:12–13, ESV)

We have been given the task of discipling the world, and within that task we have each been given smaller tasks—raising our children, doing our jobs, writing our words, scrubbing our toilets, so that *everything* in life is brought into joyful alignment with the Spirit of God—but our tasks are couched in our identities, in God's love and vision for us, in our new life as children of God.

Yes, we must disciple the world. But first we must be disciples. We must spread the message. But first we must embrace it—and find, within it, our identity, our purpose, and our relationship with our Father and his Son Jesus, the King of the Universe—and the King, if we'll allow him, of our hearts.

Rachel would love to hear from you!

You can visit her and interact online:

Web: www.rachelstarrthomson.com
Facebook.com/RachelStarrThomsonWriter
Twitter: @writerstarr

FEARLESS

You can live free from fear.

Fear steals our lives from us. It steals our impact and cripples our joy.

In our modern world, there are a million reasons to be afraid.

But what if your default mode was courage and faith, not fear and timidity?

True freedom is possible— through the presence of Jesus and the practice of his Word.

In this book, we expose the insidious roots of fear and explore the answers found in the Bible. Learn how:

- THE FEAR OF THE LORD WILL BREAK THE POWER OF LESSER FEARS

- HOLINESS WILL CHANGE YOUR IDENTITY— AND GIVE YOU COURAGE TO STAND AGAINST THE TIDE

- THE PRESENCE OF GOD IS THE ANSWER TO THE WORLD'S TROUBLES

- YOU CAN PRACTICE THE GIFTS OF POWER, LOVE, AND A SOUND MIND

Available from Amazon and everywhere books are sold.

THE SEVENTH WORLD TRILOGY

For five hundred years the Seventh World has been ruled by a tyrannical empire—and the mysterious Order of the Spider that hides in its shadow. History and truth are deliberately buried, the beauty and treachery of the past remembered only by wandering Gypsies, persecuted scholars, and a few unusual seekers. But the past matters, as Maggie Sheffield soon finds out. It matters because its forces will soon return and claim lordship over her world, for good or evil.

The Seventh World Trilogy is an epic fantasy, beautiful, terrifying, pointing to the realities just beyond the world we see.

"An excellent read, solidly recommended for fantasy readers."
– MIDWEST BOOK REVIEW

"A wonderfully realistic fantasy world. Recommended."
– JILL WILLIAMSON, CHRISTY-AWARD-WINNING AUTHOR
OF *BY DARKNESS HID*

"Epic, beautiful, well-written fantasy that sings of Christian truth."
– RAEL, READER

Available everywhere online or special order from your local bookstore.

THE ONENESS CYCLE

The supernatural entity called the Oneness holds the world together. *What happens if it falls apart?*

In a world where the Oneness exists, nothing looks the same. Dead men walk. Demons prowl the air. Old friends peel back their mundane masks and prove as supernatural as angels. But after centuries of battling demons and the corrupting powers of the world, the Oneness is under a new threat—its greatest threat. Because this time, the threat comes from within.

Fast-paced contemporary fantasy.

"Plot twists and lots of edge-of-your-seat action,
I had a hard time putting it down!"
—Alexis

"Finally! The kind of fiction I've been waiting for my whole life!"
—Mercy Hope, FaithTalks.com

"I sped through this short, fast-paced novel, pleased by the well-drawn characters and the surprising plot. Thomson has done a great job of portraying difficult emotional journeys . . . Read it!"
—Phyllis Wheeler, The Christian Fantasy Review

Available everywhere online or special order from your local bookstore.

TIME TO ALIGN:
FREE EMAIL COURSE

Join Rachel Starr Thomson and the 1:11 team for a personal journey through 8 key areas of life in our free email-based course, "Time to Align."

This free, 11-week course is a spiritual recalibration: a chance to bring your heart, soul, mind, and strength into alignment with the nature and will of God.

To get your first lesson straight to your inbox, sign up here:
One11Ministries.com/Align

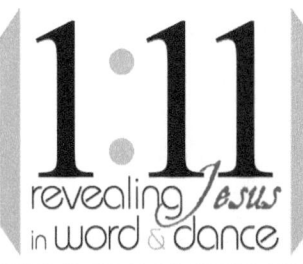

1:11 MINISTRIES
WORD. DANCE. MUSIC.

Live productions, events, and books
to inspire and empower the body of Christ.

*Learn how you can bring Rachel and the 1:11 Ministries
team to your church, conference or event at:*

one11ministries.com

www.ingramcontent.com/pod-product-compliance
Lightning Source LLC
Chambersburg PA
CBHW030117100526
44591CB00009B/432